INTRODUCTORY

ILLUSTRATED COURSE GUIDES

MICROSOFT® OFFICE 365™

EXCEL® 2016

INTRODUCTORY

ILLUSTRATED COURSE GUIDES

MICROSOFT® OFFICE 365™

EXCEL® 2016

REDING + WERMERS

For Microsoft® Office updates, go to sam.cengage.com

CENGAGE
Learning®

Australia • Brazil • Mexico • Singapore • United Kingdom • United States

Illustrated Course Guides: Microsoft® Office 365™ & Excel® 2016—Introductory
Elizabeth Eisner Reding/Lynn Wermers

SVP, GM Science, Technology & Math: Balraj Kalsi

Senior Product Director: Kathleen McMahon

Senior Product Team Manager: Lauren Murphy

Product Team Manager: Andrea Topping

Associate Product Manager: Melissa Stehler

Senior Director, Development: Julia Caballero

Product Development Manager: Leigh Hefferon

Senior Content Developer: Christina Kling-Garrett

Developmental Editor: MT Cozzola

Product Assistant: Erica Chapman

Marketing Director: Michele McTighe

Marketing Manager: Stephanie Albracht

Marketing Coordinator: Cassie Cloutier

Production Director: Patty Stephan

Senior Content Project Manager: Stacey Lamodi

Art Director: Diana Graham

Text Designer: Joseph Lee, Black Fish Design

Cover Template Designer: Lisa Kuhn, Curio Press, LLC
www.curiopress.com

Composition: GEX Publishing Services

Cover Image: 2M media / ShutterStock.com

Printed in the United States of America
Print Number: 10   Print Year: 2020

Mac users: If you're working through this product using a Mac, some of the steps may vary. Additional information for Mac users is included with the Data Files for this product.

Some of the product names and company names used in this book have been used for identification purposes only and may be trademarks or registered trademarks of their respective manufacturers and sellers.

Windows® is a registered trademark of Microsoft Corporation. © 2012 Microsoft. Microsoft and the Office logo are either registered trademarks or trademarks of Microsoft Corporation in the United States and/or other countries. Cengage Learning is an independent entity from Microsoft Corporation and not affiliated with Microsoft in any manner. Microsoft product screenshots used with permission from Microsoft Corporation. Unless otherwise noted, all clip art is courtesy of openclipart.org.

Disclaimer: Any fictional data related to persons or companies or URLs used throughout this text is intended for instructional purposes only. At the time this text was published, any such data was fictional and not belonging to any real persons or companies.

Disclaimer: The material in this text was written using Microsoft Windows 10 Professional and Office 365 Professional Plus and was Quality Assurance tested before the publication date. As Microsoft continually updates the Windows 10 operating system and Office 365, your software experience may vary slightly from what is presented in the printed text.

Library of Congress Control Number: 2016943579
ISBN: 978-1-305-87849-5

Cengage Learning
20 Channel Center Street
Boston, MA 02210
USA

Cengage Learning is a leading provider of customized learning solutions with employees residing in nearly 40 different countries and sales in more than 125 countries around the world. Find your local representative at **www.cengage.com.**

Cengage Learning products are represented in Canada by Nelson Education, Ltd.

For your course and learning solutions, visit **www.cengage.com**

Purchase any of our products at your local college store or at our preferred online store **www.cengagebrain.com**

Brief Contents

Contents

Getting Started with Microsoft Office 2016

CASE ▶ This module introduces you to the most frequently used programs in Office, as well as common features they all share.

Module Objectives

After completing this module, you will be able to:

- Understand the Office 2016 suite
- Start an Office app
- Identify Office 2016 screen elements
- Create and save a file

- Open a file and save it with a new name
- View and print your work
- Get Help, close a file, and exit an app

Files You Will Need

OF 1-1.xlsx

Understand the Office 2016 Suite

Learning Outcomes
• Identify Office suite components
• Describe the features of each app

Microsoft Office 2016 is a group of programs—which are also called applications or apps—designed to help you create documents, collaborate with coworkers, and track and analyze information. You use different Office programs to accomplish specific tasks, such as writing a letter or producing a presentation, yet all the programs have a similar look and feel. Microsoft Office 2016 apps feature a common, context-sensitive user interface, so you can get up to speed faster and use advanced features with greater ease. The Office apps are bundled together in a group called a **suite**. The Office suite is available in several configurations, but all include Word, Excel, PowerPoint, and OneNote. Some configurations include Access, Outlook, Publisher, Skype, and OneDrive. **CASE** *As part of your job, you need to understand how each Office app is best used to complete specific tasks.*

DETAILS

The Office apps covered in this book include:

- **Microsoft Word 2016**

  When you need to create any kind of text-based document, such as a memo, newsletter, or multipage report, Word is the program to use. You can easily make your documents look great by using formatting tools and inserting eye-catching graphics. The Word document shown in **FIGURE 1-1** contains a company logo and simple formatting.

- **Microsoft Excel 2016**

  Excel is the perfect solution when you need to work with numeric values and make calculations. It puts the power of formulas, functions, charts, and other analytical tools into the hands of every user, so you can analyze sales projections, calculate loan payments, and present your findings in a professional manner. The Excel worksheet shown in **FIGURE 1-1** tracks checkbook transactions. Because Excel automatically recalculates results whenever a value changes, the information is always up to date. A chart illustrates how the monthly expenses are broken down.

- **Microsoft PowerPoint 2016**

  Using PowerPoint, it's easy to create powerful presentations complete with graphics, transitions, and even a soundtrack. Using professionally designed themes and clip art, you can quickly and easily create dynamic slide shows such as the one shown in **FIGURE 1-1**.

- **Microsoft Access 2016**

  Access is a relational database program that helps you keep track of large amounts of quantitative data, such as product inventories or employee records. The form shown in **FIGURE 1-1** can be used to generate reports on customer invoices and tours.

Microsoft Office has benefits beyond the power of each program, including:

- **Note-taking made simple; available on all devices**

  Use OneNote to take notes (organized in tabbed pages) on information that can be accessed on your computer, tablet, or phone. Share the editable results with others. Contents can include text, web page clips (using OneNote Clipper), email contents (directly inserted into a default section), photos (using Office Lens), and web pages.

- **Common user interface: Improving business processes**

  Because the Office suite apps have a similar **interface**, your experience using one app's tools makes it easy to learn those in the other apps. Office documents are **compatible** with one another, so you can easily **integrate**, or combine, elements—for example, you can add an Excel chart to a PowerPoint slide, or an Access table to a Word document.

  Most Office programs include the capability to incorporate feedback—called **online collaboration**—across the Internet or a company network.

FIGURE 1-1: Microsoft Office 2016 documents

Letter created in Word

Checkbook register created in Excel

Tourism presentation created in PowerPoint

Form created in Access

What is Office 365?

Until recently, most consumers purchased Microsoft Office in a traditional way: by buying a retail package from a store or downloading it from Microsoft.com. You can still purchase Microsoft Office 2016 in this traditional way—but you can also now purchase it as a subscription service called Microsoft Office 365, which is available in a wide variety of configurations.

Depending on which configuration you purchase, you will always have access to the most up-to-date versions of the apps in your package and, in many cases, can install these apps on multiple computers, tablets, and phones. And if you change computers or devices, you can easily uninstall the apps from an old device and install them on a new one.

Start an Office App

To get started using Microsoft Office, you need to start, or **launch**, the Office app you want to use. An easy way to start the app you want is to press the Windows key, type the first few characters of the app name you want to search for, then click the app name In the Best match list. You will discover that there are many ways to accomplish just about any Windows task; for example, you can also see a list of all the apps on your computer by pressing the Windows key, then clicking All Apps. When you see the app you want, click its name. **CASE** ▶ *You decide to familiarize yourself with Office by starting Microsoft Word.*

STEPS

1. **Click the** Start button ⊞ **on the Windows taskbar**

   The Start menu opens, listing the most used apps on your computer. You can locate the app you want to open by clicking the app name if you see it, or you can type the app name to search for it.

2. **Type** word

   Your screen now displays "Word 2016" under "Best match", along with any other app that has "word" as part of its name (such as WordPad). See **FIGURE 1-2**.

3. **Click** Word 2016

   Word 2016 launches, and the Word **start screen** appears, as shown in **FIGURE 1-3**. The start screen is a landing page that appears when you first start an Office app. The left side of this screen displays recent files you have opened. (If you have never opened any files, then there will be no files listed under Recent.) The right side displays images depicting different templates you can use to create different types of documents. A **template** is a file containing professionally designed content and formatting that you can easily customize for your own needs. You can also start from scratch using the Blank Document template, which contains only minimal formatting settings.

Enabling touch mode

If you are using a touch screen with any of the Office 2016 apps, you can enable the touch mode to give the user interface a more spacious look, making it easier to navigate with your fingertips. Enable touch mode by clicking the Quick Access toolbar list arrow, then clicking Touch/Mouse Mode to select it. Then you'll see the Touch Mode button 🖐 in the Quick Access toolbar. Click 🖐, and you'll see the interface spread out.

Using shortcut keys to move between Office programs

You can switch between open apps using a keyboard shortcut. The [Alt][Tab] keyboard combination lets you either switch quickly to the next open program or file or choose one from a gallery. To switch immediately to the next open program or file, press [Alt][Tab]. To choose from all open programs and files, press and hold [Alt], then press and release [Tab] without releasing [Alt]. A gallery opens on screen, displaying the filename and a thumbnail image of each open program and file, as well as of the desktop. Each time you press [Tab] while holding [Alt], the selection cycles to the next open file or location. Release [Alt] when the program, file, or location you want to activate is selected.

FIGURE 1-2: Searching for the Word app

Word 2016 app appears as
a search result when you
type "word"

Your list may differ

FIGURE 1-3: Word start screen

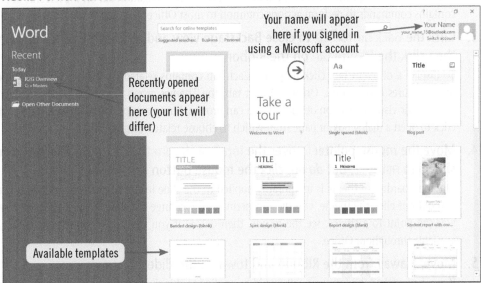

Your name will appear
here if you signed in
using a Microsoft account

Recently opened
documents appear
here (your list will
differ)

Available templates

Using the Office Clipboard

You can use the Office Clipboard to cut and copy items from one Office program and paste them into others. The Office Clipboard can store a maximum of 24 items. To access it, open the Office Clipboard task pane by clicking the dialog box launcher 🔲 in the Clipboard group on the Home tab. Each time you copy a selection, it is saved in the Office Clipboard. Each entry in the Office Clipboard includes an icon that tells you the program it was created in. To paste an entry, click in the document where you want it to appear, then click the item in the Office Clipboard. To delete an item from the Office Clipboard, right-click the item, then click Delete.

Identify Office 2016 Screen Elements

Learning Outcomes
- Identify basic components of the user interface
- Display and use Backstage view
- Adjust the zoom level

One of the benefits of using Office is that its apps have much in common, making them easy to learn and making it simple to move from one to another. All Office 2016 apps share a similar user interface, so you can use your knowledge of one to get up to speed in another. A **user interface** is a collective term for all the ways you interact with a software program. The user interface in Office 2016 provides intuitive ways to choose commands, work with files, and navigate in the program window. **CASE** *Familiarize yourself with some of the common interface elements in Office by examining the PowerPoint program window.*

STEPS

1. **Click the Start button ⊞ on the Windows taskbar, type** pow, **click** PowerPoint 2016, **then click** Blank Presentation

   PowerPoint starts and opens a new file, which contains a blank slide. Refer to **FIGURE 1-4** to identify common elements of the Office user interface. The **document window** occupies most of the screen. At the top of every Office program window is a **title bar** that displays the document name and program name. Below the title bar is the **Ribbon**, which displays commands you're likely to need for the current task. Commands are organized onto **tabs**. The tab names appear at the top of the Ribbon, and the active tab appears in front. The **Share button** in the upper-right corner lets you invite other users to view your cloud-stored Word, Excel, or Powerpoint file.

2. **Click the** File tab

   The File tab opens, displaying **Backstage view**. It is called Backstage view because the commands available here are for working with the files "behind the scenes." The navigation bar on the left side of Backstage view contains commands to perform actions common to most Office programs.

3. **Click the** Back button ⊙ **to close Backstage view and return to the document window, then click the** Design tab **on the Ribbon**

   To display a different tab, click its name. Each tab contains related commands arranged into **groups** to make features easy to find. On the Design tab, the Themes group displays available design themes in a **gallery**, or visual collection of choices you can browse. Many groups contain a **launcher**, which you can click to open a dialog box or pane from which to choose related commands.

4. **Move the mouse pointer ▷ over the** Ion Boardroom theme **in the Themes group as shown in** FIGURE 1-5, **but** *do not click* **the mouse button**

   The Ion Boardroom theme is temporarily applied to the slide in the document window. However, because you did not click the theme, you did not permanently change the slide. With the **Live Preview** feature, you can point to a choice, see the results, then decide if you want to make the change. Live Preview is available throughout Office.

5. **Move ▷ away from the Ribbon and towards the slide**

   If you had clicked the Ion theme, it would be applied to this slide. Instead, the slide remains unchanged.

6. **Point to the** Zoom slider `– ——— | — + 100%` **on the status bar, then drag to the right until the Zoom level reads** 166%

   The slide display is enlarged. Zoom tools are located on the status bar. You can drag the slider or click the Zoom In or Zoom Out buttons to zoom in or out on an area of interest. **Zooming in** (a higher percentage), makes a document appear bigger on screen but less of it fits on the screen at once; **zooming out** (a lower percentage) lets you see more of the document at a reduced size.

7. **Click the** Zoom Out button `–` **on the status bar to the left of the Zoom slider until the Zoom level reads** 120%

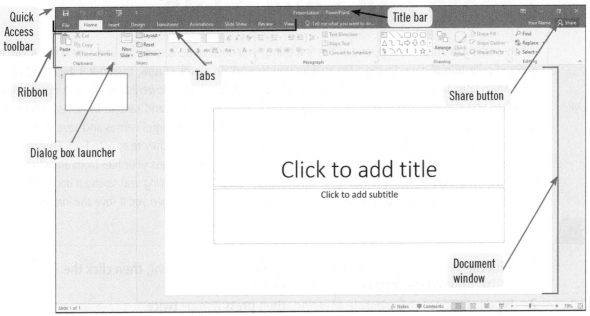

FIGURE 1-4: PowerPoint program window

Quick Access toolbar
Ribbon
Dialog box launcher
Tabs
Title bar
Share button
Click to add title
Click to add subtitle
Document window

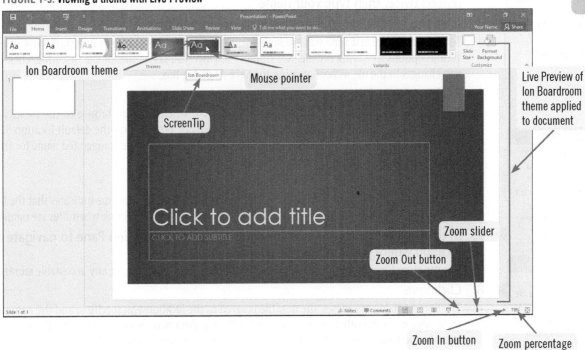

FIGURE 1-5: Viewing a theme with Live Preview

Ion Boardroom theme
Mouse pointer
ScreenTip
Live Preview of Ion Boardroom theme applied to document
Click to add title
CLICK TO ADD SUBTITLE
Zoom slider
Zoom Out button
Zoom In button
Zoom percentage

Using Backstage view

Backstage view in each Microsoft Office app offers "one stop shopping" for many commonly performed tasks, such as opening and saving a file, printing and previewing a document, defining document properties, sharing information, and exiting a program. Backstage view opens when you click the File tab in any Office app, and while features such as the Ribbon, Mini toolbar, and Live Preview all help you work *in* your documents, the File tab and Backstage view help you work *with* your documents. You can click commands in the navigation pane to open different places for working with your documents, such as the Open place, the Save place, and so on. You can return to your active document by clicking the Back button.

Create and Save a File

Learning Outcomes
• Create a file
• Save a file
• Explain OneDrive

When working in an Office app, one of the first things you need to do is to create and save a file. A **file** is a stored collection of data. Saving a file enables you to work on a project now, then put it away and work on it again later. In some Office programs, including Word, Excel, and PowerPoint, you can open a new file when you start the app, then all you have to do is enter some data and save it. In Access, you must create a file before you enter any data. You should give your files meaningful names and save them in an appropriate location, such as a folder on your hard drive or OneDrive so they're easy to find. **OneDrive** is a Microsoft cloud storage system that lets you easily save, share, and access your files from anywhere you have Internet access. **CASE** *Use Word to familiarize yourself with creating and saving a document. First you'll type some notes about a possible location for a corporate meeting, then you'll save the information for later use.*

STEPS

1. **Click the** Word button ⬚ **on the taskbar, click** Blank document, **then click the** Zoom In **button** ➕ **until the level is** 120%, **if necessary**

2. **Type** Locations for Corporate Meeting, **then press [Enter] twice**
   The text appears in the document window, and the **insertion point** blinks on a new blank line. The insertion point indicates where the next typed text will appear.

QUICK TIP
A filename can be up to 255 characters, including a file extension, and can include upper- or lowercase characters and spaces, but not ?, ", /, \, <, >, *, |, or :.

3. **Type** Las Vegas, NV, **press [Enter], type** Chicago, IL, **press [Enter], type** Seattle, WA, **press [Enter] twice, then type your name**

4. **Click the** Save button 🖫 **on the Quick Access toolbar**
   Because this is the first time you are saving this new file, the Save place in Backstage view opens, showing various options for saving the file. See **FIGURE 1-6**. Once you save a file for the first time, clicking 🖫 saves any changes to the file *without* opening the Save As dialog box.

5. **Click** Browse
   The Save As dialog box opens, as shown in **FIGURE 1-7**, where you can browse to the location where you want to save the file. The Address bar in the Save As dialog box displays the default location for saving the file, but you can change it to any location. The File name field contains a suggested name for the document based on text in the file, but you can enter a different name.

QUICK TIP
Saving a file to the Desktop creates a desktop icon that you can double-click to both launch a program and open a document.

6. **Type** OF 1-Possible Corporate Meeting Locations
   The text you type replaces the highlighted text. (The "OF 1-" in the filename indicates that the file is created in Office Module 1. You will see similar designations throughout this book when files are named.)

7. **In the Save As dialog box, use the Address bar or Navigation Pane to navigate to the location where you store your Data Files**
   You can store files on your computer, a network drive, your OneDrive, or any acceptable storage device.

QUICK TIP
To create a new blank file when a file is open, click the File tab, click New on the navigation bar, then choose a template.

8. **Click** Save
   The Save As dialog box closes, the new file is saved to the location you specified, and the name of the document appears in the title bar, as shown in **FIGURE 1-8**. (You may or may not see the file extension ".docx" after the filename.) See **TABLE 1-1** for a description of the different types of files you create in Office, and the file extensions associated with each.

TABLE 1-1: Common filenames and default file extensions

file created in	is called a	and has the default extension
Word	document	.docx
Excel	workbook	.xlsx
PowerPoint	presentation	.pptx
Access	database	.accdb

FIGURE 1-6: Save place in Backstage view

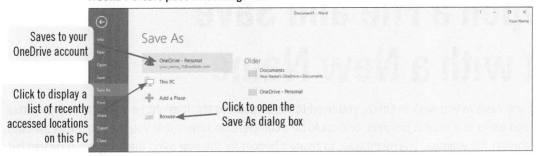

Saves to your OneDrive account

Click to display a list of recently accessed locations on this PC

Click to open the Save As dialog box

FIGURE 1-7: Save As dialog box

Address bar; your location may differ

Navigation pane; your links and folders may differ

File name field; your computer may not display file extensions

Save as type list

FIGURE 1-8: Saved and named Word document

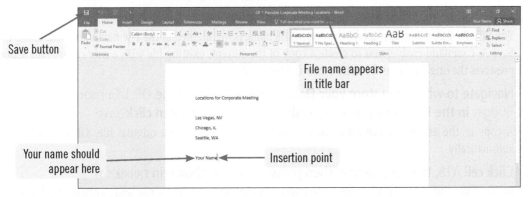

Save button

File name appears in title bar

Your name should appear here

Insertion point

Saving files to OneDrive

All Office programs include the capability to incorporate feedback—called **online collaboration**—across the Internet or a company network. Using **cloud computing** (work done in a virtual environment), you can store your work in the cloud. Using OneDrive, a file storage service from Microsoft, you and your colleagues can create and store documents in the cloud and make the documents available anywhere there is Internet access to whomever you choose. To use OneDrive, you need a Microsoft Account, which you obtain at onedrive.live.com. Pricing and storage plans vary based on the type of Microsoft account you have. When you are logged into your Microsoft account and you

save a file in any of the Office apps, the first option in the Save As screen is your OneDrive. Double-click your OneDrive option, and the Save As dialog box opens displaying a location in the address bar unique to your OneDrive account. Type a name in the File name text box, then click Save and your file is saved to your OneDrive. To sync your files with OneDrive, you'll need to download and install the OneDrive for Windows app. Then, when you open Explorer, you'll notice a new folder called OneDrive has been added to your folder. In this folder is a sub-folder called Documents. This means if your Internet connection fails, you can work on your files offline.

Office 2016
Module 1

Learning
Outcomes
• Open an existing
  file
• Save a file with a
  new name

Open a File and Save It with a New Name

In many cases as you work in Office, you need to use an existing file. It might be a file you or a coworker created earlier as a work in progress, or it could be a complete document that you want to use as the basis for another. For example, you might want to create a budget for this year using the budget you created last year; instead of typing in all the categories and information from scratch, you could open last year's budget, save it with a new name, and just make changes to update it for the current year. By opening the existing file and saving it with the Save As command, you create a duplicate that you can modify to suit your needs, while the original file remains intact. **CASE** ▸ *Use Excel to open an existing workbook file, and save it with a new name so the original remains unchanged.*

STEPS

1. **Click the** Start button ▦ **on the Windows taskbar, type** exc, **click** Excel 2016, **click** Open Other Workbooks, This PC, **then click** Browse

    The Open dialog box opens, where you can navigate to any drive or folder accessible to your computer to locate a file.

2. **In the Open dialog box, navigate to the location where you store your Data Files**

    The files available in the current folder are listed, as shown in **FIGURE 1-9**. This folder displays one file.

3. **Click** OF 1-1.xlsx, **then click** Open

    The dialog box closes, and the file opens in Excel. An Excel file is an electronic spreadsheet, so the new file displays a grid of rows and columns you can use to enter and organize data.

4. **Click the** File tab, **click** Save As **on the navigation bar, then click** Browse

    The Save As dialog box opens, and the current filename is highlighted in the File name text box. Using the Save As command enables you to create a copy of the current, existing file with a new name. This action preserves the original file and creates a new file that you can modify.

5. **Navigate to where you store your Data Files if necessary, type** OF 1-Corporate Meeting Budget **in the File name text box, as shown in FIGURE 1-10, then click** Save

    A copy of the existing workbook is created with the new name. The original file, OF 1-1.xlsx, closes automatically.

6. **Click cell** A18, **type your name, then press** [Enter], **as shown in FIGURE 1-11**

    In Excel, you enter data in cells, which are formed by the intersection of a row and a column. Cell A18 is at the intersection of column A and row 18. When you press [Enter], the cell pointer moves to cell A19.

7. **Click the** Save button ▣ **on the Quick Access toolbar**

    Your name appears in the workbook, and your changes to the file are saved.

Exploring File Open options

You might have noticed that the Open button in the Open dialog box includes a list arrow to the right of the button. In a dialog box, if a button includes a list arrow you can click the button to invoke the command, or you can click the list arrow to see a list of related commands that you can apply to the currently selected file. The Open list arrow includes several related commands, including Open Read-Only and Open as Copy.

Clicking Open Read-Only opens a file that you can only save with a new name; you cannot make changes to the original file. Clicking Open as Copy creates and opens a copy of the selected file and inserts the word "Copy" in the file's title. Like the Save As command, these commands provide additional ways to use copies of existing files while ensuring that original files do not get changed by mistake.

FIGURE 1-9: Open dialog box

FIGURE 1-10: Save As dialog box

FIGURE 1-11: Your name added to the workbook

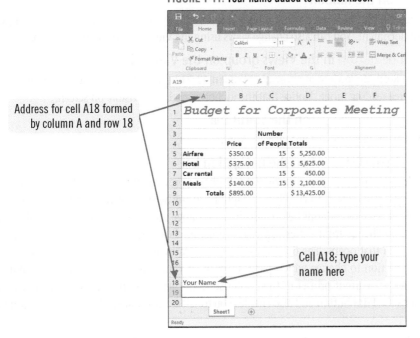

Working in Compatibility Mode

Not everyone upgrades to the newest version of Office. As a general rule, new software versions are **backward compatible**, meaning that documents saved by an older version can be read by newer software. To open documents created in older Office versions, Office 2016 includes a feature called Compatibility Mode. When you use Office 2016 to open a file created in an earlier version of Office, "Compatibility Mode" appears in the title bar, letting you know the file was created in an earlier but usable version of the program. If you are working with someone who may not be using the newest version of the software, you can avoid possible incompatibility problems by saving your file in another, earlier format. To do this in an Office program, click the File tab, click Save As on the navigation bar, then click Browse. In the Save As dialog box, click the Save as type list arrow in the Save As dialog box, then click an option in the list. For example, if you're working in Excel, click Excel 97-2003 Workbook format in the Save as type list to save an Excel file so it can be opened in Excel 97 or Excel 2003.

View and Print Your Work

Learning
Outcomes
• Describe and
  change views in
  an app
• Print a document

Each Microsoft Office program lets you switch among various **views** of the document window to show more or fewer details or a different combination of elements that make it easier to complete certain tasks, such as formatting or reading text. Changing your view of a document does not affect the file in any way, it affects only the way it looks on screen. If your computer is connected to a printer or a print server, you can easily print any Office document using the Print button in the Print place in Backstage view. Printing can be as simple as **previewing** the document to see exactly what the printed version will look like and then clicking the Print button. Or, you can customize the print job by printing only selected pages. You can also use the Share place in Backstage view or the Share button on the Ribbon (if available) to share a document, export to a different format, or save it to the cloud. **CASE** ▶ *Experiment with changing your view of a Word document, and then preview and print your work.*

STEPS

1. **Click the** Word program button 🔲 **on the taskbar**

   Word becomes active, and the program window fills the screen.

QUICK TIP

To minimize the display of the buttons and commands on tabs, click the Collapse the Ribbon button 🔼 on the lower-right end of the Ribbon.

2. **Click the** View tab **on the Ribbon**

   In most Office programs, the View tab on the Ribbon includes groups and commands for changing your view of the current document. You can also change views using the View buttons on the status bar.

3. **Click the** Read Mode button **in the Views group on the View tab**

   The view changes to Read Mode view, as shown in **FIGURE 1-12**. This view shows the document in an easy-to-read, distraction-free reading mode. Notice that the Ribbon is no longer visible on screen.

QUICK TIP

Office 2016 apps default to print to OneDrive.

4. **Click the** Print Layout button 🔲 **on the Status bar**

   You return to Print Layout view, the default view in Word.

5. **Click the** File tab, **then click** Print **on the navigation bar**

   The Print place opens. The preview pane on the right displays a preview of how your document will look when printed. Compare your screen to **FIGURE 1-13**. Options in the Settings section enable you to change margins, orientation, and related options before printing. To change a setting, click it, and then click a new setting. For instance, to change from Letter paper size to Legal, click Letter in the Settings section, then click Legal on the menu that opens. The document preview updates as you change the settings. You also can use the Settings section to change which pages to print. If your computer is connected to multiple printers, you can click the current printer in the Printer section, then click the one you want to use. The Print section contains the Print button and also enables you to select the number of copies of the document to print.

QUICK TIP

You can add the Quick Print button 🔲 to the Quick Access toolbar by clicking the Customize Quick Access Toolbar button, then clicking Quick Print. The Quick Print button prints one copy of your document using the default settings.

6. **If your school allows printing, click the** Print button **in the Print place (otherwise, click the** Back button ⬅)

   If you chose to print, a copy of the document prints, and Backstage view closes.

Customizing the Quick Access toolbar

You can customize the Quick Access toolbar to display your favorite commands. To do so, click the Customize Quick Access Toolbar button 🔽 in the title bar, then click the command you want to add. If you don't see the command in the list, click More Commands to open the Quick Access Toolbar tab of the current program's Options dialog box. In the Options dialog box, use the Choose commands from list to choose a category, click the desired command in the list on the left, click Add to add it to the

Quick Access toolbar, then click OK. To remove a button from the toolbar, click the name in the list on the right in the Options dialog box, then click Remove. To add a command to the Quick Access toolbar as you work, simply right-click the button on the Ribbon, then click Add to Quick Access Toolbar on the shortcut menu. To move the Quick Access toolbar below the Ribbon, click the Customize Quick Access Toolbar button, and then click Show Below the Ribbon.

FIGURE 1-12: Read Mode view

Las Vegas, NV
Chicago, IL
Seattle, WA

Your Name

Print Layout button

View buttons on status bar

FIGURE 1-13: Print settings on the File tab

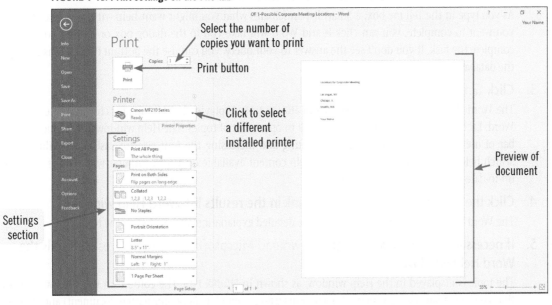

Select the number of copies you want to print

Print button

Click to select a different installed printer

Preview of document

Settings section

Creating a screen capture

A **screen capture** is a digital image of your screen, as if you took a picture of it with a camera. For instance, you might want to take a screen capture if an error message occurs and you want a Technical Support person to see exactly what's on the screen. You can create a screen capture using the Snipping Tool, an accessory designed to capture whole screens or portions of screens. To open the Snipping Tool, click the Start button on the Windows taskbar, type "sni", then click the Snipping Tool when it appears in the left panel. On the Snipping Tool toolbar, click New, then drag the pointer on the screen to select the area of the screen you want to capture. When you release the mouse button, the screen capture opens in the Snipping Tool window, and you can

save, copy, or send it in an email. In Word, Excel, and PowerPoint 2016, you can capture screens or portions of screens and insert them in the current document using the Screenshot button in the Illustrations group on the Insert tab. Alternatively, you can create a screen capture by pressing [PrtScn]. (Keyboards differ, but you may find the [PrtScn] button in or near your keyboard's function keys.) Pressing this key places a digital image of your screen in the Windows temporary storage area known as the **Clipboard**. Open the document where you want the screen capture to appear, click the Home tab on the Ribbon (if necessary), then click the Paste button in the Clipboard group on the Home tab. The screen capture is pasted into the document.

Learning
Outcomes
• Display a
  ScreenTip
• Use Help
• Close a file
• Exit an app

Get Help, Close a File, and Exit an App

You can get comprehensive help at any time by pressing [F1] in an Office app or clicking the Help button on the title bar. You can also get help in the form of a ScreenTip by pointing to almost any icon in the program window. When you're finished working in an Office document, you have a few choices for ending your work session. You close a file by clicking the File tab, then clicking Close; you exit a program by clicking the Close button on the title bar. Closing a file leaves a program running, while exiting a program closes all the open files in that program as well as the program itself. In all cases, Office reminds you if you try to close a file or exit a program and your document contains unsaved changes. **CASE** *Explore the Help system in Microsoft Office, and then close your documents and exit any open programs.*

STEPS

1. **Point to the Zoom button in the Zoom group on the View tab of the Ribbon**
   A ScreenTip appears that describes how the Zoom button works and explains where to find other zoom controls.

2. **Click the Tell me box above the Ribbon, then type Choose a template**
   As you type in the Tell me box, a Smart list anticipates what you might want help with. If you see the task you want to complete, you can click it and Word will take you to the dialog box or options you need to complete the task. If you don't see the answer to your query, you can use the bottom two options to search the database.

3. **Click Get Help on "choose a template"**
   The Word Help window opens, as shown in **FIGURE 1-14**, displaying help results for choosing a template in Word. Each entry is a hyperlink you can click to open a list of topics. The Help window also includes a toolbar of useful Help commands such as printing and increasing the font size for easier readability, and a Search field. Office.com supplements the help content available on your computer with a wide variety of up-to-date topics, templates, and training.

4. **Click the Where do I find templates link in the results list Word Help window**
   The Word Help window changes, and a more detailed explanation appears below the topic.

5. **If necessary, scroll down until the Download Microsoft Office templates topic fills the Word Help window**
   The topic is displayed in the Help window, as shown in **FIGURE 1-15**. The content in the window explains that you can create a wide variety of documents using a template (a pre-formatted document) and that you can get many templates free of charge.

6. **Click the Keep Help on Top button 📌 in the lower-right corner of the window**
   The Pin Help button rotates so the pin point is pointed towards the bottom of the screen: this allows you to read the Help window while you work on your document.

7. **Click the Word document window, notice the Help window remains visible**

8. **Click a blank area of the Help window, click 📌 to Unpin Help, click the Close button ☒ in the Help window, then click the Close button ☒ in the Word program window**
   Word closes, and the Excel program window is active.

9. **Click the Close button ☒ in the Excel program window, click the PowerPoint app button 🔳 on the taskbar if necessary, then click the Close button ☒ to exit PowerPoint**
   Excel and PowerPoint both close.

FIGURE 1-14: Word Help window

Search field

Word 2016 Help

Choose a template

Help toolbar

Click to learn how to find templates

Where do I find templates?
In Microsoft templates all the formatting is complete; ... click My Templates or Personal, and then choose your template. ... Download Microsoft Office templates.

Edit templates
Edit templates. Whether you're starting from a built-in template or updating one of your own, Word's built-in tools help you update templates to suit your needs.

Create forms that users complete or print in Word
Create forms that users complete or print in Word. You can create a form in Microsoft Word by starting with a template and ... you want people to choose a ...

Zoom in or out of a document
Choose a particular zoom setting. You can choose how

Help topics are updated frequently; your list may differ

FIGURE 1-15: Create a document Help topic

Word 2016 Help

Print button

Choose a template

Download Microsoft Office templates

Do you want to create a resume, mailing label, budget, fax cover sheet, presentation, or invitation? To get free templates like these, go to **File** > **New** in your Office program, and then click a category under **Office.com Templates**, such as **Letters**, **Business**, or **Form** (In Office 2013 or Office 2016, try one of the **Suggested searches** links).

Or, type what you're looking for in the search box, such as **avery** for labels.

TIP If you're on the web, try the free online templates at templates.office.com. You can use them right in your browser, in the Office Online programs.

Drag scroll bar to read more

Keep Help on Top button

Using sharing features and co-authoring capabilities

If you are using Word, Excel, or PowerPoint, you can take advantage of the Share feature, which makes it easy to share your files that have been saved to OneDrive. When you click the Share button, you will be asked to invite others to share the file. To do this, type in the name or email addresses in the Invite people text box. When you invite others, you have the opportunity to give them different levels of permission. You might want some people to have read-only privileges; you might want others to be able to make edits. Also available in Word, Excel, and PowerPoint is real-time co-authoring capabilities for files stored on OneDrive. Once a file on OneDrive is opened and all the users have been given editing privileges, all the users can make edits simultaneously. On first use, each user will be prompted to automatically share their changes.

Recovering a document

Each Office program has a built-in recovery feature that allows you to open and save files that were open at the time of an interruption such as a power failure. When you restart the program(s) after an interruption, the Document Recovery task pane opens on the left side of your screen displaying both original and recovered versions of the files that were open. If you're not sure which file to open (original or recovered), it's usually better to open the recovered file because it will contain the latest information. You can, however, open and review all versions of the file that were recovered and save the best one. Each file listed in the Document Recovery task pane displays a list arrow with options that allow you to open the file, save it as is, delete it, or show repairs made to it during recovery.

Practice

Concepts Review

Label the elements of the program window shown in FIGURE 1-16.

FIGURE 1-16

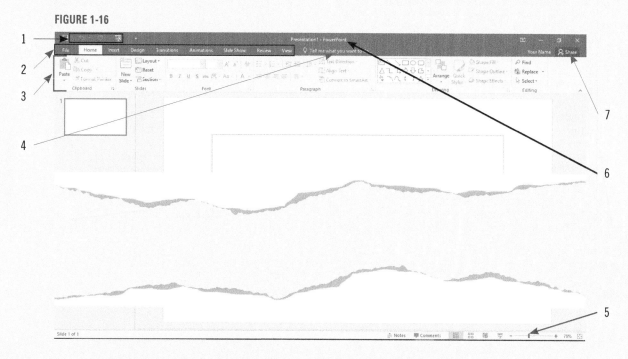

Match each project with the program for which it is best suited.

8. Microsoft PowerPoint	a. Corporate convention budget with expense projections
9. Microsoft Word	b. Presentation for city council meeting
10. Microsoft Excel	c. Business cover letter for a job application
11. Microsoft Access	d. Department store inventory

Independent Challenge 1

You just accepted an administrative position with a local independently owned insurance agent who has recently invested in computers and is now considering purchasing a subscription to Office 365. You have been asked to think of uses for the apps and you put your ideas in a Word document.

a. Start Word, create a new Blank document, then save the document as **OF 1-Microsoft Office Apps Uses** in the location where you store your Data Files.

b. Change the zoom factor to 120%, type **Microsoft Access**, press [Enter] twice, type **Microsoft Excel**, press [Enter] twice, type **Microsoft PowerPoint**, press [Enter] twice, type **Microsoft Word**, press [Enter] twice, then type your name.

c. Click the line beneath each program name, type at least two tasks you can perform using that program (each separated by a comma), then press [Enter].

d. Save the document, then submit your work to your instructor as directed.

e. Exit Word.

Getting Started with Microsoft Office 2016

Getting Started with Excel 2016

CASE You have been hired as an assistant at Reason2Go (R2G), a company that allows travelers to make a difference in the global community through voluntourism, while having a memorable vacation experience. You report to Yolanda Lee, the vice president of finance. As Yolanda's assistant, you create worksheets to analyze data from various divisions of the company, so you can help her make sound decisions on company expansion, investments, and new voluntourism opportunities.

Module Objectives

After completing this module, you will be able to:

- Understand spreadsheet software
- Identify Excel 2016 window components
- Understand formulas
- Enter labels and values and use the AutoSum button

- Edit cell entries
- Enter and edit a simple formula
- Switch worksheet views
- Choose print options

Files You Will Need

EX 1-1.xlsx   EX 1-4.xlsx
EX 1-2.xlsx   EX 1-5.xlsx
EX 1-3.xlsx

Understand Spreadsheet Software

Learning Outcomes
• Describe the uses of Excel
• Define key spreadsheet terms

Microsoft Excel is the electronic spreadsheet program within the Microsoft Office suite. An **electronic spreadsheet** is an app you use to perform numeric calculations and to analyze and present numeric data. One advantage of a spreadsheet program over pencil and paper is that your calculations are updated automatically, so you can change entries without having to manually recalculate. TABLE 1-1 shows some of the common business tasks people accomplish using Excel. In Excel, the electronic spreadsheet you work in is called a **worksheet**, and it is contained in a file called a **workbook**, which has the file extension .xlsx. **CASE** At R2G, you use Excel extensively to track finances and manage corporate data.

DETAILS

When you use Excel, you have the ability to:

• **Enter data quickly and accurately**

With Excel, you can enter information faster and more accurately than with pencil and paper. FIGURE 1-1 shows a payroll worksheet created using pencil and paper. FIGURE 1-2 shows the same worksheet created using Excel. Equations were added to calculate the hours and pay. You can use Excel to recreate this information for each week by copying the worksheet's structure and the information that doesn't change from week to week, then entering unique data and formulas for each week.

• **Recalculate data easily**

Fixing typing errors or updating data is easy in Excel. In the payroll example, if you receive updated hours for an employee, you just enter the new hours and Excel recalculates the pay.

• **Perform what-if analysis**

The ability to change data and quickly view the recalculated results gives you the power to make informed business decisions. For instance, if you're considering raising the hourly rate for an entry-level tour guide from $12.50 to $15.00, you can enter the new value in the worksheet and immediately see the impact on the overall payroll as well as on the individual employee. Any time you use a worksheet to ask the question "What if?" you are performing **what-if analysis**. Excel also includes a Scenario Manager where you can name and save different what-if versions of your worksheet.

• **Change the appearance of information**

Excel provides powerful features, such as the Quick Analysis tool, for making information visually appealing and easier to understand. Format text and numbers in different fonts, colors, and styles to make it stand out.

• **Create charts**

Excel makes it easy to create charts based on worksheet information. Charts are updated automatically in Excel whenever data changes. The worksheet in FIGURE 1-2 includes a 3-D pie chart.

• **Share information**

It's easy for everyone at R2G to collaborate in Excel using the company intranet, the Internet, or a network storage device. For example, you can complete the weekly payroll that your boss, Yolanda Lee, started creating. You can also take advantage of collaboration tools such as shared workbooks so that multiple people can edit a workbook simultaneously.

• **Build on previous work**

Instead of creating a new worksheet for every project, it's easy to modify an existing Excel worksheet. When you are ready to create next week's payroll, you can open the file for last week's payroll, save it with a new filename, and modify the information as necessary. You can also use predesigned, formatted files called **templates** to create new worksheets quickly. Excel comes with many templates that you can customize.

FIGURE 1-1: Traditional paper worksheet

Reason2Go
Project Leader Divison Payroll Calculator

Name	Hours	O/T Hrs	Hrly Rate	Reg Pay	O/T Pay	Gross Pay
Brucker, Pieter	40	4	16.75	670	134	804
Cucci, Lucia	35	0	12	420	0	420
Klimt, Gustave	40	2	13.25	530	53	583
Lafontaine, Jeanne	29	0	15.25	442.25	0	442.25
Martinez, Juan	37	0	13.2	488.4	0	488.4
Mioshi, Keiko	39	0	21	819	0	819
Shernwood, Burt	40	0	16.75	670	0	670
Strano, Riccardo	40	8	16.25	650	260	910
Wadsworth, Alice	40	5	13.25	530	132.5	662.5
Yamamoto, Johji	38	0	15.5	589	0	589

FIGURE 1-2: Excel worksheet

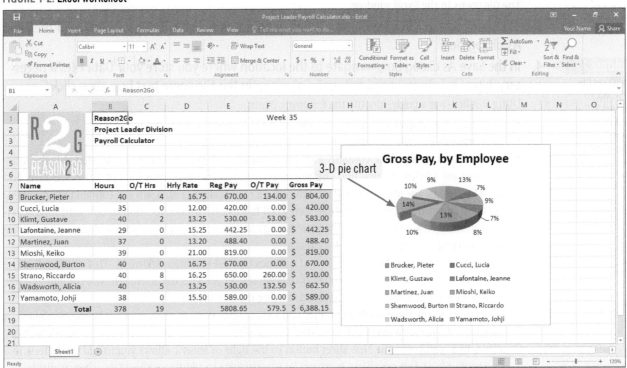

TABLE 1-1: Business tasks you can accomplish using Excel

you can use spreadsheets to	by
Perform calculations	Adding formulas and functions to worksheet data; for example, adding a list of sales results or calculating a car payment
Represent values graphically	Creating charts based on worksheet data; for example, creating a chart that displays expenses
Generate reports	Creating workbooks that combine information from multiple worksheets, such as summarized sales information from multiple stores
Organize data	Sorting data in ascending or descending order; for example, alphabetizing a list of products or customer names, or prioritizing orders by date
Analyze data	Creating data summaries and short lists using PivotTables or AutoFilters; for example, making a list of the top 10 customers based on spending habits
Create what-if data scenarios	Using variable values to investigate and sample different outcomes, such as changing the interest rate or payment schedule on a loan

Identify Excel 2016 Window Components

Learning
Outcomes
• Open and save an
Excel file
• Identify Excel
window elements

To start Excel, Microsoft Windows must be running. Similar to starting any app in Office, you can use the Start button on the Windows taskbar, the Start button on your keyboard, or you may have a shortcut on your desktop you prefer to use. If you need additional assistance, ask your instructor or technical support person. **CASE** *You decide to start Excel and familiarize yourself with the worksheet window.*

STEPS

QUICK TIP

For more information on starting a program or opening and saving a file, see the module "Getting Started with Microsoft Office 2016."

1. **Start Excel, click** Open Other Workbooks **on the navigation bar, click** This PC, **then click** Browse **to open the Open dialog box**

2. **In the Open dialog box, navigate to the location where you store your Data Files, click** EX 1-1.xlsx, **then click** Open
   The file opens in the Excel window.

3. **Click the** File tab, **click** Save As **on the navigation bar, then click** Browse **to open the Save As dialog box**

TROUBLE

If you don't see the extension .xlsx on the filenames in the Save As dialog box, don't worry; Windows can be set up to display or not to display the file extensions.

4. **In the Save As dialog box, navigate to the location where you store your Data Files if necessary, type** EX 1-Project Leader Payroll Calculator **in the File name text box, then click** Save
   Using **FIGURE 1-3** as a guide, identify the following items:
   - The **Name box** displays the active cell address. "A1" appears in the Name box.
   - The **formula bar** allows you to enter or edit data in the worksheet.
   - The **worksheet window** contains a grid of columns and rows. Columns are labeled alphabetically and rows are labeled numerically. The worksheet window can contain a total of 1,048,576 rows and 16,384 columns. The intersection of a column and a row is called a **cell**. Cells can contain text, numbers, formulas, or a combination of all three. Every cell has its own unique location or **cell address**, which is identified by the coordinates of the intersecting column and row. The column and row indicators are shaded to make identifying the cell address easy.
   - The **cell pointer** is a dark rectangle that outlines the cell you are working in. This cell is called the **active cell**. In **FIGURE 1-3**, the cell pointer outlines cell A1, so A1 is the active cell. The column and row headings for the active cell are highlighted, making it easier to locate.
   - **Sheet tabs** below the worksheet grid let you switch from sheet to sheet in a workbook. By default, a workbook file contains one worksheet—but you can have as many sheets as your computer's memory allows, in a workbook. The New sheet button to the right of Sheet 1 allows you to add worksheets to a workbook. **Sheet tab scrolling buttons** let you navigate to additional sheet tabs when available.
   - You can use the **scroll bars** to move around in a worksheet that is too large to fit on the screen at once.
   - The **status bar** is located at the bottom of the Excel window. It provides a brief description of the active command or task in progress. **The mode indicator** in the lower-left corner of the status bar provides additional information about certain tasks.

5. **Click cell** A4
   Cell A4 becomes the active cell. To activate a different cell, you can click the cell or press the arrow keys on your keyboard to move to it.

QUICK TIP

The button that displays in the bottom-right corner of a range is the Quick Analysis tool.

6. **Click cell** B5, **press and hold the mouse button, drag** ✛ **to cell** B14, **then release the mouse button**
   You selected a group of cells and they are highlighted, as shown in **FIGURE 1-4**. A selection of two or more cells such as B5:B14 is called a **range**; you select a range when you want to perform an action on a group of cells at once, such as moving them or formatting them. When you select a range, the status bar displays the average, count (or number of items selected), and sum of the selected cells as a quick reference.

FIGURE 1-3: Open workbook

FIGURE 1-4: Selected range

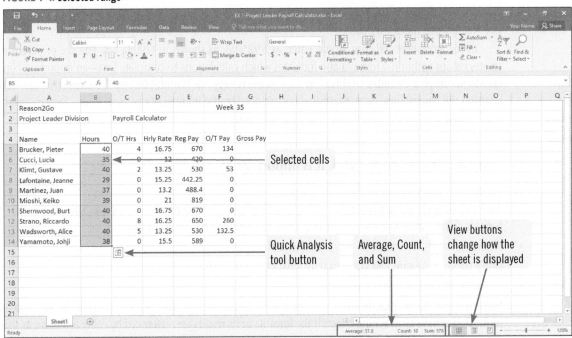

Using OneDrive and Office Online

If you have a Microsoft account, you can save your Excel files and photos in OneDrive, a cloud-based service from Microsoft. When you save files in OneDrive, you can access them on other devices—such as a tablet or smartphone. OneDrive is available as an app on smartphones and tablets, making access simple. You can open files to view

them on any device, and you can even make edits to them using **Office Online**, which includes simplified versions of the apps found in the Office 2016 suite. Because Office Online is web-based, the apps take up no computer disk space and you can use them on any Internet-connected device.

Understand Formulas

Learning
Outcomes
• Explain how a
  formula works
• Identify Excel
  arithmetic operators

Excel is a truly powerful program because users at every level of mathematical expertise can make calculations with accuracy. To do so, you use formulas. A **formula** is an equation in a worksheet. You use formulas to make calculations as simple as adding a column of numbers, or as complex as creating profit-and-loss projections for a global corporation. To tap into the power of Excel, you should understand how formulas work. **CASE** *Managers at R2G use the Project Leader Payroll Calculator workbook to keep track of employee hours prior to submitting them to the Payroll Department. You'll be using this workbook regularly, so you need to understand the formulas it contains and how Excel calculates the results.*

STEPS

1. **Click cell E5**

   The active cell contains a formula, which appears on the formula bar. All Excel formulas begin with the equal sign (=). If you want a cell to show the result of adding 4 plus 2, the formula in the cell would look like this: =4+2. If you want a cell to show the result of multiplying two values in your worksheet, such as the values in cells B5 and D5, the formula would look like this: =B5*D5, as shown in **FIGURE 1-5**. While you're entering a formula in a cell, the cell references and arithmetic operators appear on the formula bar. See **TABLE 1-2** for a list of commonly used arithmetic operators. When you're finished entering the formula, you can either click the Enter button on the formula bar or press [Enter].

2. **Click cell F5**

   This cell contains an example of a more complex formula, which calculates overtime pay. At R2G, overtime pay is calculated at twice the regular hourly rate times the number of overtime hours. The formula used to calculate overtime pay for the employee in row 5 is:

   O/T Hrs times (2 times Hrly Rate)

   In the worksheet cell, you would enter: =C5*(2*D5), as shown in **FIGURE 1-6**. The use of parentheses creates groups within the formula and indicates which calculations to complete first—an important consideration in complex formulas. In this formula, first the hourly rate is multiplied by 2, because that calculation is within the parentheses. Next, that value is multiplied by the number of overtime hours. Because overtime is calculated at twice the hourly rate, managers are aware that they need to closely watch this expense.

DETAILS

In creating calculations in Excel, it is important to:

• **Know where the formulas should be**

  An Excel formula is created in the cell where the formula's results should appear. This means that the formula calculating Gross Pay for the employee in row 5 will be entered in cell G5.

• **Know exactly what cells and arithmetic operations are needed**

  Don't guess; make sure you know exactly what cells are involved before creating a formula.

• **Create formulas with care**

  Make sure you know exactly what you want a formula to accomplish before it is created. An inaccurate formula may have far-reaching effects if the formula or its results are referenced by other formulas, as shown in the payroll example in **FIGURE 1-6**.

• **Use cell references rather than values**

  The beauty of Excel is that whenever you change a value in a cell, any formula containing a reference to that cell is automatically updated. For this reason, it's important that you use cell references in formulas, rather than actual values, whenever possible.

• **Determine what calculations will be needed**

  Sometimes it's difficult to predict what data will be needed within a worksheet, but you should try to anticipate what statistical information may be required. For example, if there are columns of numbers, chances are good that both column and row totals should be present.

FIGURE 1-5: Viewing a formula

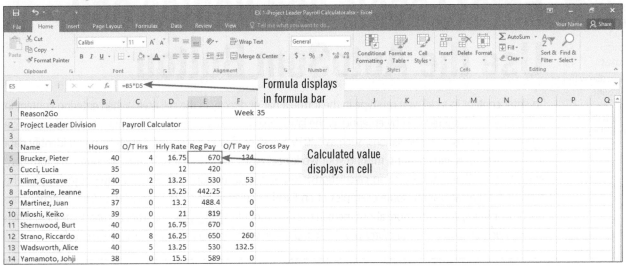

Formula displays in formula bar

Calculated value displays in cell

FIGURE 1-6: Formula with multiple operators

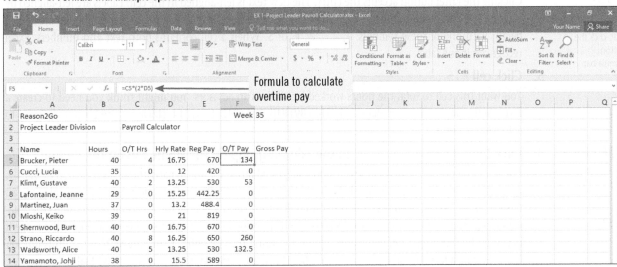

Formula to calculate overtime pay

TABLE 1-2: Excel arithmetic operators

operator	purpose	example
+	Addition	=A5+A7
-	Subtraction or negation	=A5-10
*	Multiplication	=A5*A7
/	Division	=A5/A7
%	Percent	=35%
^ (caret)	Exponent	=6^2 (same as 6^2)

Enter Labels and Values and Use the AutoSum Button

Learning Outcomes
• Build formulas with the AutoSum button
• Copy formulas with the fill handle

To enter content in a cell, you can type in the formula bar or directly in the cell itself. When entering content in a worksheet, you should start by entering all the labels first. **Labels** are entries that contain text and numerical information not used in calculations, such as "2019 Sales" or "Travel Expenses". Labels help you identify data in worksheet rows and columns, making your worksheet easier to understand. **Values** are numbers, formulas, and functions that can be used in calculations. To enter a calculation, you type an equal sign (=) plus the formula for the calculation; some examples of an Excel calculation are "=2+2" and "=C5+C6". Functions are built-in formulas; you learn more about them in the next module. **CASE** *You want to enter some information in the Project Leader Payroll Calculator workbook and use a very simple function to total a range of cells.*

STEPS

1. **Click cell A15, then click in the formula bar**

   Notice that the **mode indicator** on the status bar now reads "Edit," indicating you are in Edit mode. You are in Edit mode any time you are entering or changing the contents of a cell.

QUICK TIP
If you change your mind and want to cancel an entry in the formula bar, click the Cancel button ✕ on the formula bar.

2. **Type Totals, then click the Enter button ✓ on the formula bar**

   Clicking the Enter button accepts the entry. The new text is left-aligned in the cell. Labels are left-aligned by default, and values are right-aligned by default. Excel recognizes an entry as a value if it is a number or it begins with one of these symbols: +, -, =, @, #, or $. When a cell contains both text and numbers, Excel recognizes it as a label.

3. **Click cell B15**

   You want this cell to total the hours worked by all the trip advisors. You might think you need to create a formula that looks like this: =B5+B6+B7+B8+B9+B10+B11+B12+B13+B14. However, there's an easier way to achieve this result.

QUICK TIP
The AutoSum button is also referred to as the Sum button because clicking it inserts the SUM function.

4. **Click the AutoSum button Σ in the Editing group on the Home tab on the Ribbon**

   The SUM function is inserted in the cell, and a suggested range appears in parentheses, as shown in **FIGURE 1-7**. A **function** is a built-in formula; it includes the **arguments** (the information necessary to calculate an answer) as well as cell references and other unique information. Clicking the AutoSum button sums the adjacent range (that is, the cells next to the active cell) above or to the left, although you can adjust the range if necessary by selecting a different range before accepting the cell entry. Using the SUM function is quicker than entering a formula, and using the range B5:B14 is more efficient than entering individual cell references.

QUICK TIP
You can create formulas in a cell even before you enter the values to be calculated.

5. **Click ✓ on the formula bar**

   Excel calculates the total contained in cells B5:B14 and displays the result, 378, in cell B15. The cell actually contains the formula =SUM(B5:B14), and the result is displayed.

6. **Click cell C13, type 6, then press [Enter]**

   The number 6 replaces the cell's contents, the cell pointer moves to cell C14, and the value in cell F13 changes.

QUICK TIP
You can also press [Tab] to complete a cell entry and move the cell pointer to the right.

7. **Click cell C18, type Average Gross Pay, then press [Enter]**

   The new label is entered in cell C18. The contents appear to spill into the empty cells to the right.

8. **Click cell B15, position the pointer on the lower-right corner of the cell (the fill handle) so that the pointer changes to +, drag + to cell G15, then release the mouse button**

   Dragging the fill handle across a range of cells copies the contents of the first cell into the other cells in the range. In the range B15:G15, each filled cell now contains a function that sums the range of cells above, as shown in **FIGURE 1-8**.

9. **Save your work**

Getting Started with Excel 2016

FIGURE 1-7: Creating a formula using the AutoSum button

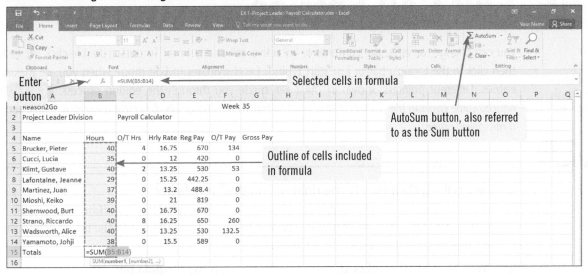

FIGURE 1-8: Results of copied SUM functions

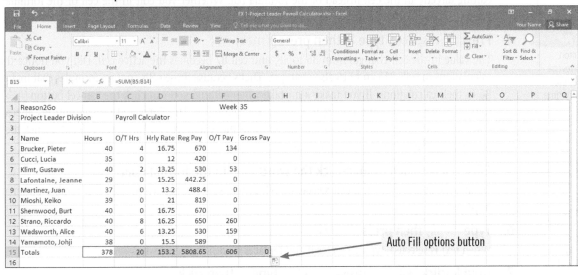

Navigating a worksheet

With over a million cells available in a worksheet, it is important to know how to move around in, or **navigate**, a worksheet. You can use the arrow keys on the keyboard ↑, ↓, →, or ← to move one cell at a time, or press [Page Up] or [Page Down] to move one screen at a time. To move one screen to the left, press [Alt][Page Up]; to move one screen to the right, press [Alt][Page Down]. You can also use the mouse pointer to click the desired cell. If the desired cell is not visible in the worksheet window, use the scroll bars or use the Go To command by clicking the Find & Select button in the Editing group on the Home tab on the Ribbon. To quickly jump to the first cell in a worksheet, press [Ctrl][Home]; to jump to the last cell, press [Ctrl][End].

Edit Cell Entries

Learning Outcomes
• Edit cell entries in the formula bar
• Edit cell entries in the cell

You can change, or **edit**, the contents of an active cell at any time. To do so, double-click the cell, and then click in the formula bar or just start typing. Excel switches to Edit mode when you are making cell entries. Different pointers, shown in TABLE 1-3, guide you through the editing process. **CASE** *You noticed some errors in the worksheet and want to make corrections. The first error is in cell A5, which contains a misspelled name.*

STEPS

1. **Click cell A5, then click to the right of P in the formula bar**

   As soon as you click in the formula bar, a blinking vertical line called the **insertion point** appears on the formula bar at the location where new text will be inserted. See FIGURE 1-9. The mouse pointer changes to Ⲓ when you point anywhere in the formula bar.

2. **Press [Delete], then click the Enter button ✓ on the formula bar**

   Clicking the Enter button accepts the edit, and the spelling of the employee's first name is corrected. You can also press [Enter] or [Tab] to accept an edit. Pressing [Enter] to accept an edit moves the cell pointer down one cell, and pressing [Tab] to accept an edit moves the cell pointer one cell to the right.

   > **QUICK TIP**
   > On some keyboards, you might need to press an [F-Lock] key to enable the function keys.

3. **Click cell B6, then press [F2]**

   Excel switches to Edit mode, and the insertion point blinks in the cell. Pressing [F2] activates the cell for editing directly in the cell instead of the formula bar. Whether you edit in the cell or the formula bar is simply a matter of preference; the results in the worksheet are the same.

   > **QUICK TIP**
   > The Undo button allows you to reverse up to 100 previous actions, one at a time.

4. **Press [Backspace], type 8, then press [Enter]**

   The value in the cell changes from 35 to 38, and cell B7 becomes the active cell. Did you notice that the calculations in cells B15 and E15 also changed? That's because those cells contain formulas that include cell B6 in their calculations. If you make a mistake when editing, you can click the Cancel button ✕ on the formula bar *before* pressing [Enter] to confirm the cell entry. The Enter and Cancel buttons appear only when you're in Edit mode. If you notice the mistake *after* you have confirmed the cell entry, click the Undo button ↶ on the Quick Access toolbar.

   > **QUICK TIP**
   > You can use the keyboard to select all cell contents by clicking to the right of the cell contents in the cell or formula bar, pressing and holding [Shift], then pressing [Home].

5. **Click cell A9, then double-click the word Juan in the formula bar**

   Double-clicking a word in a cell selects it. When you selected the word, the Mini toolbar automatically displayed.

6. **Type Javier, then press [Enter]**

   When text is selected, typing deletes it and replaces it with the new text.

7. **Double-click cell C12, press [Delete], type 4, then click ✓**

   Double-clicking a cell activates it for editing directly in the cell. Compare your screen to FIGURE 1-10.

8. **Save your work**

Recovering unsaved changes to a workbook file

You can use Excel's AutoRecover feature to automatically save (Autosave) your work as often as you want. This means that if you suddenly lose power or if Excel closes unexpectedly while you're working, you can recover all or some of the changes you made since you saved it last. (Of course, this is no substitute for regularly saving your work: this is just added insurance.) To customize the AutoRecover settings, click the File tab, click Options, then click

Save. AutoRecover lets you decide how often and into which location it should Autosave files. When you restart Excel after losing power, a Document Recovery pane opens and provides access to the saved and Autosaved versions of the files that were open when Excel closed. You can also click the File tab, click Open on the navigation bar, then click any file in the Recover Unsaved Workbooks list to open Autosaved workbooks.

FIGURE 1-9: Worksheet in Edit mode

FIGURE 1-10: Edited worksheet

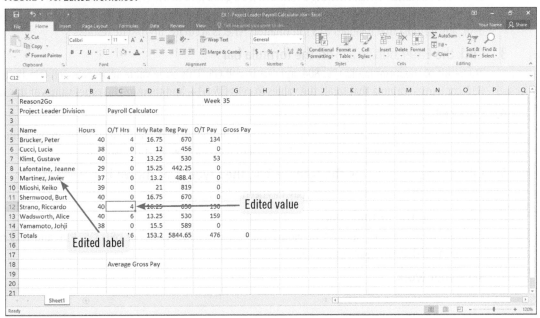

TABLE 1-3: Common pointers in Excel

name	pointer	use to	visible over the
Normal	⊹	Select a cell or range; indicates Ready mode	Active worksheet
Fill handle	✛	Copy cell contents to adjacent cells	Lower right corner of the active cell or range
I-beam	I	Edit cell contents in active cell or formula bar	Active cell in Edit mode or over the formula bar
Move	⬖	Change the location of the selected cell(s)	Perimeter of the active cell(s)
Copy	⬖⁺	Create a duplicate of the selected cell(s)	Perimeter of the active cell(s) when [Ctrl] is pressed
Column resize	↔	Change the width of a column	Border between column heading indicators

Enter and Edit a Simple Formula

Learning
Outcomes
• Enter a formula
• Use cell references
  to create a formula

You use formulas in Excel to perform calculations such as adding, multiplying, and averaging. Formulas in an Excel worksheet start with the equal sign (=), also called the **formula prefix**, followed by cell addresses, range names, values, and **calculation operators**. Calculation operators indicate what type of calculation you want to perform on the cells, ranges, or values. They can include **arithmetic operators**, which perform mathematical calculations (see TABLE 1-2 in the "Understand Formulas" lesson); **comparison operators**, which compare values for the purpose of true/false results; **text concatenation operators**, which join strings of text in different cells; and **reference operators**, which enable you to use ranges in calculations. **CASE** *You want to create a formula in the worksheet that calculates gross pay for each employee.*

STEPS

1. **Click cell G5**

   This is the first cell where you want to insert the formula. To calculate gross pay, you need to add regular pay and overtime pay. For employee Peter Brucker, regular pay appears in cell E5 and overtime pay appears in cell F5.

QUICK TIP
You can reference a
cell in a formula
either by typing the
cell reference or
clicking the cell in
the worksheet; when
you click a cell to add
a reference, the
Mode indicator
changes to "Point."

2. **Type =, click cell E5, type +, then click cell F5**

   Compare your formula bar to **FIGURE 1-11**. The blue and red cell references in cell G5 correspond to the colored cell outlines. When entering a formula, it's a good idea to use cell references instead of values whenever you can. That way, if you later change a value in a cell (if, for example, Peter's regular pay changes to 690), any formula that includes this information reflects accurate, up-to-date results.

3. **Click the Enter button ☑ on the formula bar**

   The result of the formula =E5+F5, 804, appears in cell G5. This same value appears in cell G15 because cell G15 contains a formula that totals the values in cells G5:G14, and there are no other values at this time.

4. **Click cell F5**

   The formula in this cell calculates overtime pay by multiplying overtime hours (C5) times twice the regular hourly rate (2*D5). You want to edit this formula to reflect a new overtime pay rate.

5. **Click to the right of 2 in the formula bar, then type .5 as shown in FIGURE 1-12**

   The formula that calculates overtime pay has been edited.

6. **Click ☑ on the formula bar**

   Compare your screen to **FIGURE 1-13**. Notice that the calculated values in cells G5, F15, and G15 have all changed to reflect your edits to cell F5.

7. **Save your work**

Understanding named ranges

It can be difficult to remember the cell locations of critical information in a worksheet, but using cell names can make this task much easier. You can name a single cell or range of contiguous, or touching, cells. For example, you might name a cell that contains data on average gross pay "AVG_GP" instead of trying to remember the cell address C18. A named range must begin with a letter or an underscore. It cannot contain any spaces or be the same as a built-in name, such as a function or another object (such as a different named range) in the workbook. To name a range, select the cell(s) you want to name, click the Name box in the formula bar, type the name you want to use, then press [Enter]. You can also name a range by clicking the Formulas tab, then clicking the Define Name button in the Defined Names group. Type the new range name in the Name text box in the New Name dialog box, verify the selected range, then click OK. When you use a named range in a formula, the named range appears instead of the cell address. You can also create a named range using the contents of a cell already in the range. Select the range containing the text you want to use as a name, then click the Create from Selection button in the Defined Names group. The Create Names from Selection dialog box opens. Choose the location of the name you want to use, then click OK.

FIGURE 1-11: Simple formula in a worksheet

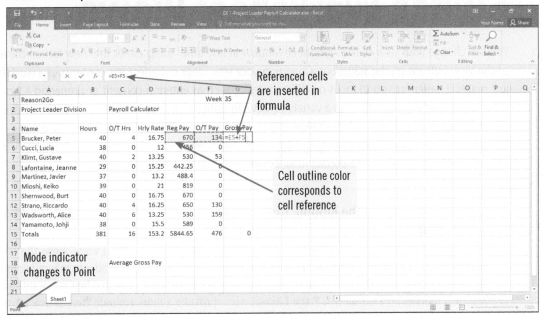

Referenced cells are inserted in formula

Cell outline color corresponds to cell reference

Mode indicator changes to Point

FIGURE 1-12: Edited formula in a worksheet

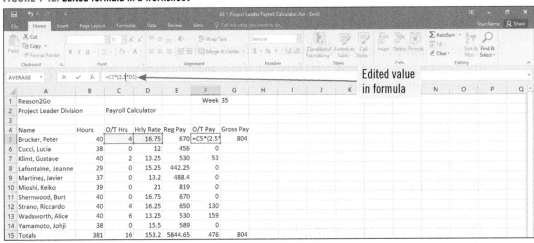

Edited value in formula

FIGURE 1-13: Edited formula with changes

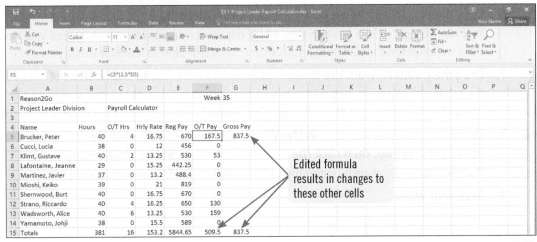

Edited formula results in changes to these other cells

Switch Worksheet Views

Learning
Outcomes
• Change worksheet
  views
• Create a header/
  footer
• Select a range

You can change your view of the worksheet window at any time, using either the View tab on the Ribbon or the View buttons on the status bar. Changing your view does not affect the contents of a worksheet; it just makes it easier for you to focus on different tasks, such as entering content or preparing a worksheet for printing. The View tab includes a variety of viewing options, such as View buttons, zoom controls, and the ability to show or hide worksheet elements such as gridlines. The status bar offers fewer View options but can be more convenient to use. **CASE** *You want to make some final adjustments to your worksheet, including adding a header so the document looks more polished.*

STEPS

QUICK TIP
Although a worksheet can contain more than a million rows and thousands of columns, the current document contains only as many pages as necessary for the current project.

1. **Click the View tab on the Ribbon, then click the Page Layout button in the Workbook Views group**

   The view switches from the default view, Normal, to Page Layout view. **Normal view** shows the worksheet without including certain details like headers and footers, or tools like rulers and a page number indicator; it's great for creating and editing a worksheet, but may not be detailed enough when you want to put the finishing touches on a document. **Page Layout view** provides a more accurate view of how a worksheet will look when printed, as shown in FIGURE 1-14. The margins of the page are displayed, along with a text box for the header. A footer text box appears at the bottom of the page, but your screen may not be large enough to view it without scrolling. Above and to the left of the page are rulers. Part of an additional page appears to the right of this page, but it is dimmed, indicating that it does not contain any data. A page number indicator on the status bar tells you the current page and the total number of pages in this worksheet.

2. **Move the pointer ⬚ over the header *without clicking***

   The header is made up of three text boxes: left, center, and right. Each text box is outlined in green as you pass over it with the pointer.

QUICK TIP
You can change header and footer information using the Header & Footer Tools Design tab that opens on the Ribbon when a header or footer is active. For example, you can insert the date by clicking the Current Date button in the Header & Footer Elements group, or insert the time by clicking the Current Time button.

3. **Click the left header text box, type Reason2Go, click the center header text box, type Project Leader Payroll Calculator, click the right header text box, then type Week 35**

   The new text appears in the text boxes, as shown in FIGURE 1-15. You can also press the [Tab] key to advance from one header box to the next.

4. **Select the range A1:G2, then press [Delete]**

   The duplicate information you just entered in the header is deleted from cells in the worksheet.

5. **Click the View tab if necessary, click the Ruler check box in the Show group, then click the Gridlines check box in the Show group**

   The rulers and the gridlines are hidden. By default, gridlines in a worksheet do not print, so hiding them gives you a more accurate image of your final document.

6. **Click the Page Break Preview button ⬚ on the status bar**

   Your view changes to Page Break Preview, which displays a reduced view of each page of your worksheet, along with page break indicators that you can drag to include more or less information on a page.

QUICK TIP
Once you view a worksheet in Page Break Preview, the page break indicators appear as dotted lines after you switch back to Normal view or Page Layout view.

7. **Drag the pointer ⬚ from the bottom page break indicator to the bottom of row 20**

   See FIGURE 1-16. When you're working on a large worksheet with multiple pages, sometimes you need to adjust where pages break; in this worksheet, however, the information all fits comfortably on one page.

8. **Click the Page Layout button in the Workbook Views group, click the Ruler check box in the Show group, then click the Gridlines check box in the Show group**

   The rulers and gridlines are no longer hidden. You can show or hide View tab items in any view.

9. **Save your work**

FIGURE 1-14: Page Layout view

Turns ruler on/off

Workbook Views group

Turns gridlines on/off

Vertical ruler

Horizontal ruler

Header text box

Additional dimmed page

Current page and total number of pages

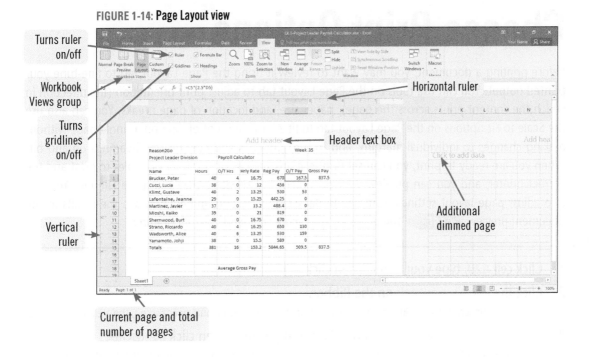

FIGURE 1-15: Header text entered

Header & Footer Tools Design tab

Header text boxes

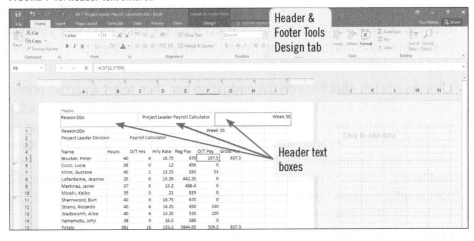

FIGURE 1-16: Page Break Preview

Blue outline indicates print area

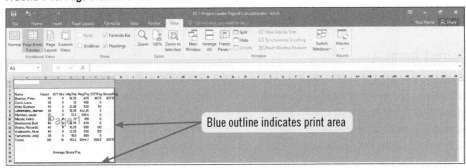

Choose Print Options

Learning
Outcomes
• Change the page
  orientation
• Hide/view gridlines
  when printing
• Preview and print
  a worksheet

Before printing a document, you may want to review it using the Page Layout tab to fine-tune your printed output. You can use tools on the Page Layout tab to adjust print orientation (the direction in which the content prints across the page), paper size, and location of page breaks. You can also use the Scale to Fit options on the Page Layout tab to fit a large amount of data on a single page without making changes to individual margins, and to turn gridlines and column/row headings on and off. When you are ready to print, you can set print options such as the number of copies to print and the correct printer, and you can preview your document in Backstage view using the File tab. You can also adjust page layout settings from within Backstage view and immediately see the results in the document preview. **CASE** *You are ready to prepare your worksheet for printing.*

STEPS

1. **Click cell A20, type your name, then click ✓**

2. **Click the Page Layout tab on the Ribbon**
   Compare your screen to **FIGURE 1-17**. The solid outline indicates the default **print area**, the area to be printed.

3. **Click the Orientation button in the Page Setup group, then click Landscape**
   The paper orientation changes to **landscape**, so the contents will print across the length of the page instead of across the width. Notice how the margins of the worksheet adjust.

4. **Click the Orientation button in the Page Setup group, then click Portrait**
   The orientation returns to **portrait**, so the contents will print across the width of the page.

5. **Click the Gridlines View check box in the Sheet Options group on the Page Layout tab, click the Gridlines Print check box to select it if necessary, then save your work**
   Printing gridlines makes the data easier to read, but the gridlines will not print unless the Gridlines Print check box is checked.

6. **Click the File tab, click Print on the navigation bar, then select an active printer if necessary**
   The Print tab in Backstage view displays a preview of your worksheet exactly as it will look when it is printed. To the left of the worksheet preview, you can also change a number of document settings and print options. To open the Page Setup dialog box and adjust page layout options, click the Page Setup link in the Settings section. Compare your preview screen to **FIGURE 1-18**. You can print from this view by clicking the Print button, or return to the worksheet without printing by clicking the Back button ⬅. You can also print an entire workbook from the Backstage view by clicking the Print button in the Settings section, then selecting the active sheet or entire workbook.

7. **Compare your settings to FIGURE 1-18, then click the Print button**
   One copy of the worksheet prints.

8. **Submit your work to your instructor as directed, then exit Excel**

Printing worksheet formulas

Sometimes you need to keep a record of all the formulas in a worksheet. You might want to do this to see exactly how you came up with a complex calculation, so you can explain it to others. To prepare a worksheet to show formulas rather than results when printed, open the workbook containing the formulas you want to print. Click the Formulas tab, then click the Show Formulas button in the Formula Auditing group to select it. When the Show Formulas button is selected, formulas rather than resulting values are displayed in the worksheet on screen and when printed. (The Show Formulas button is a toggle: click it again to hide the formulas.)

FIGURE 1-17: Worksheet with Portrait orientation

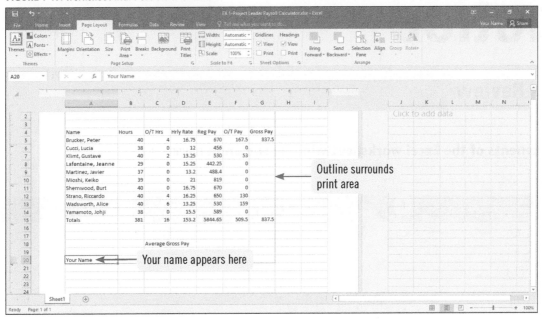

FIGURE 1-18: Worksheet in Backstage view

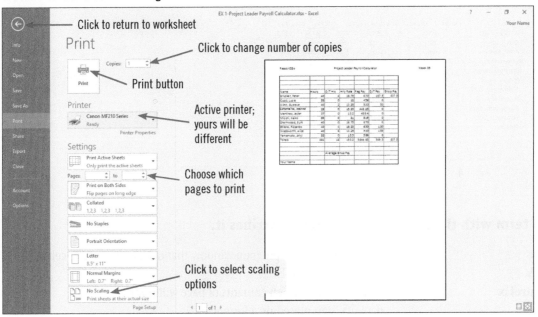

Scaling to fit

If you have a large amount of data that you want to fit to a single sheet of paper, but you don't want to spend a lot of time trying to adjust the margins and other settings, you have several options. You can easily print your work on a single sheet by clicking the No Scaling list arrow in the Settings section on the Print place in Backstage view, then clicking Fit Sheet in One Page. Another method for fitting worksheet content onto one page is to click the Page Layout tab, then change the Width and Height settings in the Scale to Fit group each to 1 Page. You can also use the Fit to option in the Page Setup dialog box to fit a worksheet on one page. To open the Page Setup dialog box, click the dialog box launcher in the Scale to Fit group on the Page Layout tab, or click the Page Setup link in the Print place in Backstage view. Make sure the Page tab is selected in the Page Setup dialog box, then click the Fit to option button.

Practice

Concepts Review

Label the elements of the Excel worksheet window shown in FIGURE 1-19.

FIGURE 1-19

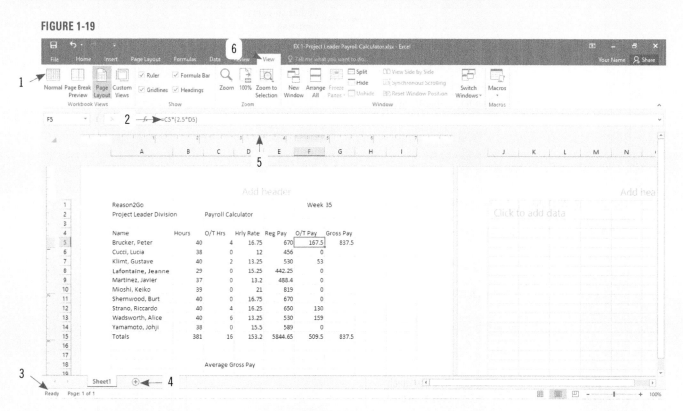

Match each term with the statement that best describes it.

7. **Name box**

8. **Workbook**

9. **Formula prefix**

10. **Orientation**

11. **Cell**

12. **Normal view**

a. Part of the Excel program window that displays the active cell address

b. Default view in Excel

c. Direction in which contents of page will print

d. Equal sign preceding a formula

e. File consisting of one or more worksheets

f. Intersection of a column and a row

Select the best answer from the list of choices.

13. **Which feature could be used to print a very long worksheet on a single sheet of paper?**
    a. Show Formulas
    b. Scale to Fit
    c. Page Break Preview
    d. Named Ranges

14. **In which area can you see a preview of your worksheet?**
    a. Page Setup
    b. Backstage view
    c. Printer Setup
    d. View tab

15. **A selection of multiple cells is called a:**
    a. Group.
    b. Range.
    c. Reference.
    d. Package.

16. **Using a cell address in a formula is known as:**
    a. Formularizing.
    b. Prefixing.
    c. Cell referencing.
    d. Cell mathematics.

17. **Which worksheet view shows how your worksheet will look when printed?**
    a. Page Layout
    b. Data
    c. Review
    d. View

18. **Which key can you press to switch to Edit mode?**
    a. [F1]
    b. [F2]
    c. [F4]
    d. [F6]

19. **In which view can you see the header and footer areas of a worksheet?**
    a. Normal view
    b. Page Layout view
    c. Page Break Preview
    d. Header/Footer view

20. **Which view shows you a reduced view of each page of your worksheet?**
    a. Normal
    b. Page Layout
    c. Thumbnail
    d. Page Break Preview

21. **The maximum number of worksheets you can include in a workbook is:**
    a. 3.
    b. 250.
    c. 255.
    d. Unlimited.

Skills Review

1. **Understand spreadsheet software.**
    a. What is the difference between a workbook and a worksheet?
    b. Identify five common business uses for electronic spreadsheets.
    c. What is what-if analysis?
2. **Identify Excel 2016 window components.**
    a. Start Excel.
    b. Open EX 1-2.xlsx from the location where you store your Data Files, then save it as **EX 1-Weather Data**.
    c. Locate the formula bar, the Sheet tabs, the mode indicator, and the cell pointer.
3. **Understand formulas.**
    a. What is the average high temperature of the listed cities? (*Hint*: Select the range B5:G5 and use the status bar.)
    b. What formula would you create to calculate the difference in altitude between Atlanta and Dallas? Enter your answer (as an equation) in cell D13.

Skills Review (continued)

4. Enter labels and values and use the AutoSum button.

   a. Click cell H8, then use the AutoSum button to calculate the total snowfall.

   b. Click cell H7, then use the AutoSum button to calculate the total rainfall.

   c. Save your changes to the file.

5. Edit cell entries.

   a. Use [F2] to correct the spelling of SanteFe in cell G3 (the correct spelling is Santa Fe).

   b. Click cell A17, then type your name.

   c. Save your changes.

6. Enter and edit a simple formula.

   a. Change the value 41 in cell C8 to **52**.

   b. Change the value 37 in cell D6 to **35.4**.

   c. Select cell J4, then use the fill handle to copy the formula in cell J4 to cells J5:J8.

   d. Save your changes.

7. Switch worksheet views.

   a. Click the View tab on the Ribbon, then switch to Page Layout view.

   b. Add the header **Average Annual Weather Data** to the center header text box.

   c. Add your name to the right header box.

   d. Delete the contents of cell A17.

   e. Delete the contents of cell A1.

   f. Save your changes.

8. Choose print options.

   a. Use the Page Layout tab to change the orientation to Portrait.

   b. Turn off gridlines by deselecting both the Gridlines View and Gridlines Print check boxes (if necessary) in the Sheet Options group.

   c. Scale the worksheet so all the information fits on one page. If necessary, scale the worksheet so all the information fits on one page. (*Hint*: Click the Width list arrow in the Scale to Fit group, click 1 page, click the Height list arrow in the Scale to Fit group, then click 1 page.) Compare your screen to **FIGURE 1-20**.

   d. Preview the worksheet in Backstage view, then print the worksheet.

   e. Save your changes, submit your work to your instructor as directed, then close the workbook and exit Excel.

FIGURE 1-20

Average Annual Weather Data   Your Name

	Atlanta	Boston	Dallas	Orlando	Phoenix	Santa Fe	Total		Average
Altitude	1050	20	430	91	1110	7000			1616.83
High Temp	89	69	96	82	86	70			82
Low Temp	33.5	44	35.4	62	59	43			46.15
Rain (in.)	50.19	42.53	21.32	47.7	7.3	14	183.04		30.5067
Snow (in.)	0	52	6	0	0	32	90		15

Alt. Diff. ->   Atlanta & Dallas   620

Independent Challenge 1

A real estate development company has hired you to help them make the transition to using Excel in their office. They would like to list properties they are interested in acquiring in a workbook. You've started a worksheet for this project that contains labels but no data.

a. Open the file EX 1-3.xlsx from the location where you store your Data Files, then save it as **EX 1-Real Estate Acquisitions**.

b. Enter the data shown in TABLE 1-4 in columns A, C, D, and E (the property address information should spill into column B).

TABLE 1-4

Property Address	Price	Bedrooms	Bathrooms	Area
1507 Pinon Lane	575000	4	2.5	NE
32 Zanzibar Way	429000	3	4	SE
60 Pottery Lane	526500	2	2	NE
902 Excelsior Drive	315000	4	3	NW

c. Use Page Layout view to create a header with the following components: the title **Real Estate Acquisitions** in the center and your name on the right.

d. Create formulas for totals in cells C6:E6.

e. Save your changes, then compare your worksheet to FIGURE 1-21.

f. Submit your work to your instructor as directed.

g. Close the worksheet and exit Excel.

FIGURE 1-21

Independent Challenge 2

You are the general manager for Luxury Motors, a high-end auto reseller. Although the company is just five years old, it is expanding rapidly, and you are continually looking for ways to save time. You recently began using Excel to manage and maintain data on inventory and sales, which has greatly helped you to track information accurately and efficiently.

a. Start Excel.

b. Save a new workbook as **EX 1-Luxury Motors** in the location where you store your Data Files.

c. Switch to an appropriate view, then add a header that contains your name in the left header text box and the title **Luxury Motors** in the center header text box.

Independent Challenge 2 (continued)

d. Using **FIGURE 1-22** as a guide, create labels for at least seven car manufacturers and sales for three months. Include other labels as appropriate. The car make should be in column A and the months should be in columns B, C, and D. A Total row should be beneath the data, and a Total column should be in column E.

FIGURE 1-22

e. Enter values of your choice for the monthly sales for each make.

f. Add formulas in the Total column to calculate total quarterly sales for each make. Add formulas at the bottom of each column of values to calculate the total for that column. Remember that you can use the AutoSum button and the fill handle to save time.

g. Save your changes, preview the worksheet in Backstage view, then submit your work to your instructor as directed.

h. Close the workbook and exit Excel.

Independent Challenge 3

This Independent Challenge requires an Internet connection.

Your company, which is headquartered in Paris, is planning to open an office in New York City. You think it would be helpful to create a worksheet that can be used to convert Celsius temperatures to Fahrenheit, to help employees who are unfamiliar with this type of temperature measurement.

a. Start Excel, then save a blank workbook as **EX 1-Temperature Conversions** in the location where you store your Data Files.

b. Create column headings using **FIGURE 1-23** as a guide. (*Hint*: You can widen column B by clicking cell B1, clicking the Format button in the Cells group on the Home tab, then clicking AutoFit Column Width.)

FIGURE 1-23

c. Create row labels for each of the seasons.

d. In the appropriate cells, enter what you determine to be a reasonable indoor temperature for each season.

e. Use your web browser to find out the conversion rate for Fahrenheit to Celsius. (*Hint*: Use your favorite search engine to search on a term such as **temperature conversion formula**.)

Independent Challenge 3 (continued)

f. In the appropriate cells, create a formula that calculates the conversion of the Fahrenheit temperature you entered into a Celsius temperature.

g. In Page Layout View, add your name and the title **Temperature Conversions** to the header.

h. Save your work, then submit your work to your instructor as directed.

i. Close the file, then exit Excel.

Independent Challenge 4: Explore

You've been asked to take over a project started by a co-worker whose Excel skills are not as good as your own. The assignment was to create a sample invoice for an existing client. The invoice will include personnel hours, supplies, and sales tax. Your predecessor started the project, including layout and initial calculations, but she has not made good use of Excel features and has made errors in her calculations. Complete the worksheet by correcting the errors and improving the design. Be prepared to discuss what is wrong with each of the items in the worksheet that you change.

a. Start Excel, open the file EX 1-4.xlsx from the location where you store your Data Files, then save it as **EX 1-Improved Invoice**.

b. There is an error in cell E5: please use the Help feature to find out what is wrong. If you need additional assistance, search Help on *overview of formulas*.

c. Correct the error in the formula in cell E5, then copy the corrected formula into cells E6:E7.

d. Correct the error in the formula in cell E11, then copy the corrected formula into cells E12 and E13.

e. Cells E8 and E14 also contain incorrect formulas. Cell E8 should contain a formula that calculates the total personnel expense, and cell E14 should calculate the total supplies used.

f. Cell G17 should contain a formula that adds the Invoice subtotal (total personnel and total supplies).

g. Cell G18 should calculate the sales tax by multiplying the Subtotal (G17) and the sales tax (cell G18).

h. The Invoice Total (cell G19) should contain a formula that adds the Invoice subtotal (cell G17) and Sales tax (cell G18).

i. Add the following to cell A21: **Terms**, then add the following to cell B21: **Net 10**.

j. Switch to Page Layout view and make the following changes to the Header: Improved Invoice for Week 22 (in the left header box), Client ABC (in the center header box), and your name (in the right header box).

k. Delete the contents of A1:A2, switch to Normal view, then compare your worksheet to FIGURE 1-24.

l. Save your work.

FIGURE 1-24

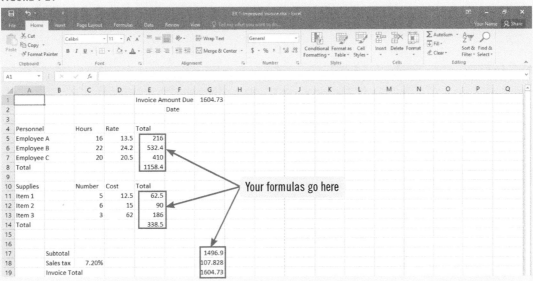

Visual Workshop

Open the file EX 1-5.xlsx from the location where you store your Data Files, then save it as **EX 1-Project Tools**. Using the skills you learned in this module, modify your worksheet so it matches **FIGURE 1-25**. Enter formulas in cells D4 through D13 and in cells B14 and C14. Use the AutoSum button and fill handle to make entering your formulas easier. Add your name in the left header text box, then print one copy of the worksheet with the formulas displayed.

FIGURE 1-25

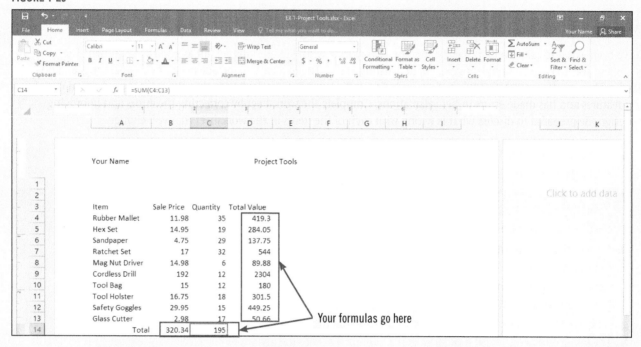

Working with Formulas and Functions

CASE ▶ Yolanda Lee, the vice president of finance at Reason2Go, needs to analyze tour expenses for the current year. She has asked you to prepare a worksheet that summarizes this expense data and includes some statistical analysis. She would also like you to perform some what-if analysis, to see what quarterly expenses would look like with various projected increases.

Module Objectives

After completing this module, you will be able to:

- Create a complex formula
- Insert a function
- Type a function
- Copy and move cell entries
- Understand relative and absolute cell references

- Copy formulas with relative cell references
- Copy formulas with absolute cell references
- Round a value with a function

Files You Will Need

EX 2-1.xlsx   EX 2-3.xlsx
EX 2-2.xlsx   EX 2-4.xlsx

Create a Complex Formula

Learning
Outcomes:
- Create a complex formula by pointing
- Use the fill handle and Auto Fill

A **complex formula** is one that uses more than one arithmetic operator. You might, for example, need to create a formula that uses addition and multiplication. In formulas containing more than one arithmetic operator, Excel uses the standard **order of precedence** rules to determine which operation to perform first. You can change the order of precedence in a formula by using parentheses around the part you want to calculate first. For example, the formula =4+2*5 equals 14, because the order of precedence dictates that multiplication is performed before addition. However, the formula =(4+2)*5 equals 30, because the parentheses cause 4+2 to be calculated first. **CASE** ▶ *You want to create a formula that calculates a 20% increase in tour expenses.*

STEPS

1. **Start Excel, open the file** EX 2-1.xlsx **from the location where you store your Data Files, then save it as** EX 2-R2G Tour Expense Analysis

2. **Select the range** B4:B11, **click the** Quick Analysis tool 📄 **that appears below the selection, then click the** Totals tab

   The Totals tab in the Quick Analysis tool displays commonly used functions, as seen in **FIGURE 2-1**.

3. **Click the** AutoSum button Σ **in the Quick Analysis tool**

   The newly calculated value displays in cell B12 and has bold formatting automatically applied, helping to set it off as a sum. This shading is temporary, and will not appear after you click a cell.

4. **Click cell** B12, **then drag the** fill handle **to cell** E12

   The formula in cell B12, as well as the bold formatting, is copied to cells C12:E12.

5. **Click cell** B14, **type** =, **click cell** B12, **then type** +

   In this first part of the formula, you are inserting a reference to the cell that contains total expenses for Quarter 1.

6. **Click cell** B12, **then type** *.2

   The second part of this formula adds a 20% increase (B12*.2) to the original value of the cell (the total expenses for Quarter 1).

7. **Click the** Enter button ✓ **on the formula bar**

   The result, 42749.58, appears in cell B14.

8. **Press [Tab], type** =, **click cell** C12, **type** +, **click cell** C12, **type** *.2, **then click** ✓

   The result, 42323.712, appears in cell C14.

9. **Drag the fill handle from cell** C14 **to cell** E14, **then save your work**

   The calculated values appear in the selected range, as shown in **FIGURE 2-2**. Dragging the fill handle on a cell copies the cell's contents or continues a series of data (such as Quarter 1, Quarter 2, etc.) into adjacent cells. This option is called **Auto Fill**.

Using Add-ins to improve worksheet functionality

Excel has more functionality than simple and complex math computations. Using the My Add-ins feature (found in the Add-ins group in the Insert tab), you can insert an add-in into your worksheet that accesses the web and adds functionality. Many of the add-ins are free or available for a small fee and can be used to create an email, appointment, meeting, contact, or task, or be a reference source, such as the Mini Calendar or Date Picker. When you click the My Add-ins button list arrow, you'll see any Recently Used Add-ins. Click See All to display the featured Add-ins for Office and to go to the Store to view available add-ins. When you find one you want, make sure you're logged in to Office.com, click the add-in, click Trust It, and the add-in will be installed. Click the My Add-ins button and your add-in should display under Recently Used Add-ins. Click it, then click Insert. The add-in will display in the Recently Used Add-ins pane when you click the My Add-ins button.

FIGURE 2-1: Totals tab in the Quick Analysis tool

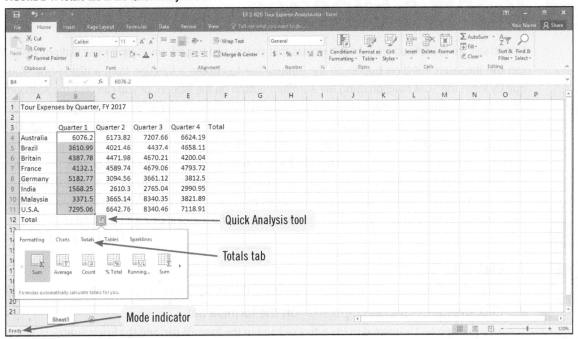

FIGURE 2-2: Results of copied formulas

Reviewing the order of precedence

When you work with formulas that contain more than one operator, the order of precedence is very important because it affects the final value. If a formula contains two or more operators, such as 4+.55/4000*25, Excel performs the calculations in a particular sequence based on the following rules: Operations inside parentheses are calculated before any other operations. Reference operators (such as ranges) are calculated first. Exponents are calculated next, then any multiplication and first. Exponents are calculated next, then any multiplication and

division—progressing from left to right. Finally, addition and subtraction are calculated from left to right. In the example 4+.55/4000*25, Excel performs the arithmetic operations by first dividing .55 by 4000, then multiplying the result by 25, then adding 4. You can change the order of calculations by using parentheses. For example, in the formula (4+.55)/4000*25, Excel would first add 4 and .55, then divide that amount by 4000, then finally multiply by 25.

Insert a Function

Learning
Outcomes
• Use the Insert
  Function button
• Select a range for
  use in a function
• Select a function
  from the AutoSum
  list arrow

Functions are predefined worksheet formulas that enable you to perform complex calculations easily. You can use the Insert Function button on the formula bar to choose a function from a dialog box. You can quickly insert the SUM function using the AutoSum button on the Ribbon, or you can click the AutoSum list arrow to enter other frequently used functions, such as **AVERAGE**. You can also use the Quick Analysis tool to calculate commonly used functions. Functions are organized into categories, such as Financial, Date & Time, and Statistical, based on their purposes. You can insert a function on its own or as part of another formula. For example, you have used the SUM function on its own to add a range of cells. You could also use the SUM function within a formula that adds a range of cells and then multiplies the total by a decimal. If you use a function alone, it always begins with an equal sign (=) as the formula prefix. **CASE** *You need to calculate the average expenses for the first quarter of the year and decide to use a function to do so.*

STEPS

1. **Click cell B15**

   This is the cell where you want to enter a calculation that averages expenses per country for the first quarter.

2. **Click the Insert Function button f_x on the formula bar**

   An equal sign (=) is inserted in the active cell and in the formula bar, and the Insert Function dialog box opens, as shown in **FIGURE 2-3**. In this dialog box, you specify the function you want to use by clicking it in the Select a function list. The Select a function list initially displays recently used functions. If you don't see the function you want, you can click the Or select a category list arrow to choose the desired category. If you're not sure which category to choose, you can type the function name or a description in the Search for a function field. The AVERAGE function is a statistical function, but you don't need to open the Statistical category because this function already appears in the Most Recently Used category.

3. **Click AVERAGE in the Select a function list if necessary, read the information that appears under the list, then click OK**

   The Function Arguments dialog box opens, in which you define the range of cells you want to average.

4. **Click the Collapse button 🔢 in the Number1 field of the Function Arguments dialog box, select the range B4:B11 in the worksheet, then click the Expand button 🔲 in the Function Arguments dialog box**

   Clicking the Collapse button minimizes the dialog box so that you can select cells in the worksheet. When you click the Expand button, the dialog box is restored, as shown in **FIGURE 2-4**. You can also begin dragging in the worksheet to automatically minimize the dialog box; after you select the desired range, the dialog box is restored.

5. **Click OK**

   The Function Arguments dialog box closes, and the calculated value is displayed in cell B15. The average expenses per country for Quarter 1 is 4453.0813.

6. **Click cell C15, click the AutoSum list arrow Σ in the Editing group on the Home tab, then click Average**

   A ScreenTip beneath cell C15 displays the arguments needed to complete the function. The text "number1" is in boldface, telling you that the next step is to supply the first cell in the group you want to average.

7. **Select the range C4:C11 in the worksheet, then click the Enter button ☑ on the formula bar**

   The average expenses per country for the second quarter appear in cell C15.

8. **Drag the fill handle from cell C15 to cell E15**

   The formula in cell C15 is copied to the rest of the selected range, as shown in **FIGURE 2-5**.

9. **Save your work**

FIGURE 2-3: Insert Function dialog box

Search for a function field →

Your list of recently used functions may differ →

Or select a category list arrow

Description of selected function

FIGURE 2-4: Expanded Function Arguments dialog box

Function in formula bar

Insert Function button

Argument

Collapse button

Sum list arrow

Drag title bar of dialog box to move it if necessary

Description of function and arguments

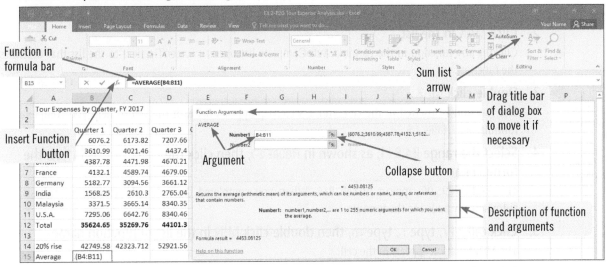

FIGURE 2-5: Average functions used in worksheet

Completed function appears in formula bar

Formula in cell C15 copied to cells D15 and E15

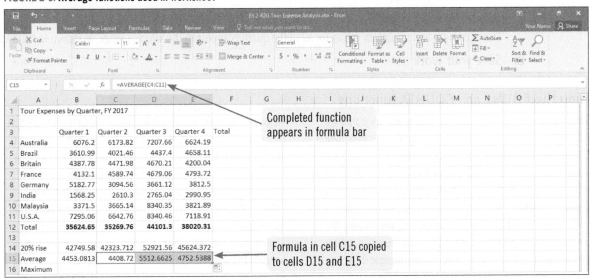

Working with Formulas and Functions

Type a Function

Learning
Outcomes
• Select a function
  by typing
• Use AutoComplete
  to copy formulas

In addition to using the Insert Function dialog box, the AutoSum button, or the AutoSum list arrow on the Ribbon to enter a function, you can manually type the function into a cell and then complete the arguments needed. This method requires that you know the name and initial characters of the function, but it can be faster than opening several dialog boxes. Experienced Excel users often prefer this method, but it is only an alternative, not better or more correct than any other method. The Excel **Formula AutoComplete** feature makes it easier to enter function names by typing, because it suggests functions depending on the first letters you type. **CASE** *You want to calculate the maximum and minimum quarterly expenses in your worksheet, and you decide to manually enter these statistical functions.*

STEPS

1. **Click cell B16, type =, then type m**

   Because you are manually typing this function, it is necessary to begin with the equal sign (=). The Formula AutoComplete feature displays a list of function names beginning with "M" beneath cell B16. Once you type an equal sign in a cell, each letter you type acts as a trigger to activate the Formula AutoComplete feature. This feature minimizes the amount of typing you need to do to enter a function and reduces typing and syntax errors.

2. **Click MAX in the list**

   Clicking any function in the Formula AutoComplete list opens a ScreenTip next to the list that describes the function.

3. **Double-click MAX**

   The function is inserted in the cell, and a ScreenTip appears beneath the cell to help you complete the formula. See **FIGURE 2-6**.

4. **Select the range B4:B11, as shown in FIGURE 2-7, then click the Enter button ✓ on the formula bar**

   The result, 7295.06, appears in cell B16. When you completed the entry, the closing parenthesis was automatically added to the formula.

5. **Click cell B17, type =, type m, then double-click MIN in the list of function names**

   The MIN function appears in the cell.

6. **Select the range B4:B11, then press [Enter]**

   The result, 1568.25, appears in cell B17.

7. **Select the range B16:B17, then drag the fill handle from cell B17 to cell E17**

   The maximum and minimum values for all of the quarters appear in the selected range, as shown in **FIGURE 2-8**.

8. **Save your work**

Using the COUNT and COUNTA functions

When you select a range, a count of cells in the range that are not blank appears in the status bar. You can use this information to determine things such as how many team members entered project hours in a worksheet. For example, if you select the range A1:A5 and only cells A1, A4, and A5 contain data, the status bar displays "Count: 3." To count nonblank cells more precisely, or to incorporate these calculations in a worksheet, you can use the COUNT and COUNTA functions. The COUNT function returns the number of cells in a range that contain numeric data, including numbers, dates, and formulas. The COUNTA function returns the number of cells in a range that contain any data at all, including numeric data, labels, and even a blank space. For example, the formula =COUNT(A1:A5) returns the number of cells in the range that contain numeric data, and the formula =COUNTA(A1:A5) returns the number of cells in the range that are not empty. If you use the COUNT functions in the Quick Analysis tool, the calculation is entered in the cell immediately beneath the selected range.

FIGURE 2-6: MAX function in progress

13					
14	20% rise	42749.58	42323.712	52921.56	45624.372
15	Average	4453.0813	4408.72	5512.6625	4752.5388
16	Maximum	=MAX(			
17	Minimum	MAX(**number1**, [number2], ...)			

FIGURE 2-7: Completing the MAX function

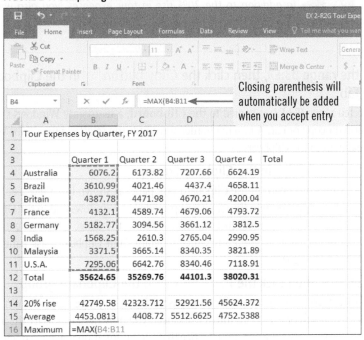

FIGURE 2-8: Completed MAX and MIN functions

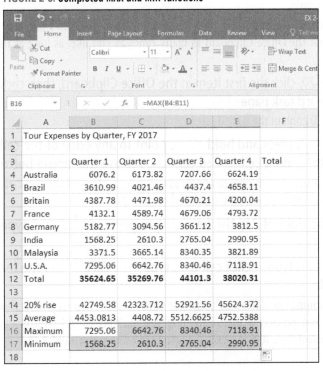

Copy and Move Cell Entries

Learning
Outcomes
• Copy a range to
  the Clipboard
• Paste a Clipboard
  entry
• Empty cell contents
• Copy cell contents

There are three ways you can copy or move cells and ranges (or the contents within them) from one location to another: the Cut, Copy, and Paste buttons on the Home tab on the Ribbon; the fill handle in the lower-right corner of the active cell or range; or the drag-and-drop feature. When you copy cells, the original data remains in the original location; when you cut or move cells, the original data is deleted from its original location. You can also cut, copy, and paste cells or ranges from one worksheet to another. **CASE** ➤ *In addition to the 20% rise in tour expenses, you also want to show a 30% rise. Rather than retype this information, you copy and move selected cells.*

STEPS

QUICK TIP
To cut or copy selected cell contents, activate the cell, then select the characters within the cell that you want to cut or copy.

1. **Select the range B3:E3, then click the Copy button 📋 in the Clipboard group on the Home tab**

   The selected range (B3:E3) is copied to the **Clipboard**, a temporary Windows storage area that holds the selections you copy or cut. A moving border surrounds the selected range until you press [Esc] or copy an additional item to the Clipboard.

2. **Click the launcher 🔲 in the Clipboard group**

   The Office Clipboard opens in the Clipboard task pane, as shown in **FIGURE 2-9**. When you copy or cut an item, it is cut or copied both to the Clipboard provided by Windows and to the Office Clipboard. Unlike the Windows Clipboard, which holds just one item at a time, the Office Clipboard contains up to 24 of the most recently cut or copied items from any Office program. Your Clipboard task pane may contain more items than shown in the figure.

QUICK TIP
Once the Office Clipboard contains 24 items, the oldest existing item is automatically deleted each time you add an item.

3. **Click cell B19, then click the Paste button in the Clipboard group**

   A copy of the contents of range B3:E3 is pasted into the range B19:E19. When pasting an item from the Office Clipboard or Clipboard into a worksheet, you only need to specify the upper left cell of the range where you want to paste the selection. Notice that the information you copied remains in the original range B3:E3; if you had cut instead of copied, the information would have been deleted from its original location once it was pasted.

4. **Press [Delete]**

   The selected cells are empty. You have decided to paste the cells in a different row. You can repeatedly paste an item from the Office Clipboard as many times as you like, as long as the item remains in the Office Clipboard.

QUICK TIP
You can also close the Office Clipboard pane by clicking the launcher in the Clipboard group.

5. **Click cell B20, click the first item in the Office Clipboard, then click the Close button ✕ on the Clipboard task pane**

   Cells B20:E20 contain the copied labels.

6. **Click cell A14, press and hold [Ctrl], point to any edge of the cell until the pointer changes to ↖, drag cell A14 to cell A21, release the mouse button, then release [Ctrl]**

   The copy pointer ↖ continues to appear as you drag, as shown in **FIGURE 2-10**. When you release the mouse button, the contents of cell A14 are copied to cell A21.

7. **Click to the right of 2 in the formula bar, press [Backspace], type 3, then click the Enter button ✓**

8. **Click cell B21, type =, click cell B12, type *1.3, click ✓ on the formula bar, then save your work**

   This new formula calculates a 30% increase of the expenses for Quarter 1, though using a different method from what you previously used. Anything you multiply by 1.3 returns an amount that is 130% of the original amount, or a 30% increase. Compare your screen to **FIGURE 2-11**.

FIGURE 2-9: Copied data in Office Clipboard

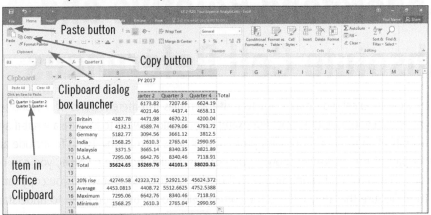

FIGURE 2-10: Copying cell contents with drag-and-drop

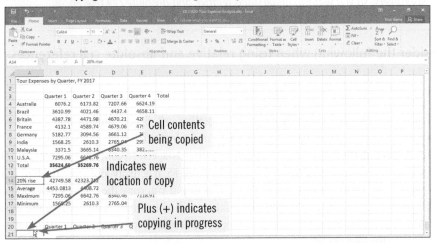

FIGURE 2-11: Formula entered to calculate a 30% increase

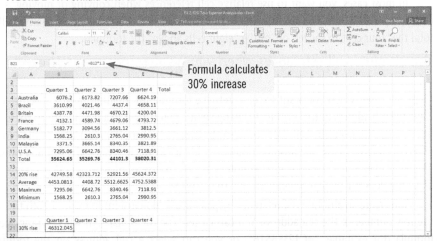

Inserting and deleting selected cells

As you add formulas to your workbook, you may need to insert or delete cells. When you do this, Excel automatically adjusts cell references to reflect their new locations. To insert cells, click the Insert list arrow in the Cells group on the Home tab, then click Insert Cells. The Insert dialog box opens, asking if you want to insert a cell and move the current active cell down or to the right of the new one. To delete one or more selected cells, click the Delete list arrow in the Cells group, click Delete Cells, and in the Delete dialog box, indicate which way you want to move the adjacent cells. When using this option, be careful not to disturb row or column alignment that may be necessary to maintain the accuracy of cell references in the worksheet. Click the Insert button or Delete button in the Cells group to insert or delete a single cell.

Understand Relative and Absolute Cell References

Learning
Outcomes
• Identify cell
  referencing
• Identify when to
  use absolute or
  relative cell
  references

As you work in Excel, you may want to reuse formulas in different parts of a worksheet to reduce the amount of data you have to retype. For example, you might want to include a what-if analysis in one part of a worksheet showing a set of sales projections if sales increase by 10%. To include another analysis in another part of the worksheet showing projections if sales increase by 50%, you can copy the formulas from one section to another and simply change the "1" to a "5". But when you copy formulas, it is important to make sure that they refer to the correct cells. To do this, you need to understand the difference between relative and absolute cell references. **CASE** ▶ *You plan to reuse formulas in different parts of your worksheets, so you want to understand relative and absolute cell references.*

DETAILS

Consider the following when using relative and absolute cell references:

• **Use relative references when you want to preserve the relationship to the formula location**

When you create a formula that references another cell, Excel normally does not "record" the exact cell address for the cell being referenced in the formula. Instead, it looks at the relationship that cell has to the cell containing the formula. For example, in **FIGURE 2-12**, cell F5 contains the formula: =SUM(B5:E5). When Excel retrieves values to calculate the formula in cell F5, it actually looks for "the four cells to the left of the formula," which in this case is cells B5:E5. This way, if you copy the cell to a new location, such as cell F6, the results will reflect the new formula location and will automatically retrieve the values in cells B6, C6, D6, and E6. These are **relative cell references**, because Excel is recording the input cells *in relation to* or *relative to* the formula cell.

In most cases, you want to use relative cell references when copying or moving, so this is the Excel default. In **FIGURE 2-12**, the formulas in cells F5:F12 and cells B13:F13 contain relative cell references. They total the "four cells to the left of" or the "eight cells above" the formulas.

• **Use absolute cell references when you want to preserve the exact cell address in a formula**

There are times when you want Excel to retrieve formula information from a specific cell, and you don't want the cell address in the formula to change when you copy it to a new location. For example, you might have a price in a specific cell that you want to use in all formulas, regardless of their location. If you use relative cell referencing, the formula results would be incorrect, because the formula would reference a different cell every time you copy it. Therefore, you need to use an **absolute cell reference**, which is a reference that does not change when you copy the formula.

You create an absolute cell reference by placing a $ (dollar sign) in front of both the column letter and the row number of the cell address. You can either type the dollar sign when typing the cell address in a formula (for example, "=C12*$B$16") or you can select a cell address on the formula bar and then press [F4], and the dollar signs are added automatically. **FIGURE 2-13** shows formulas containing both absolute and relative references. The formulas in cells B19 to E26 use absolute cell references to refer to a potential sales increase of 50%, shown in cell B16.

FIGURE 2-12: Formulas containing relative references

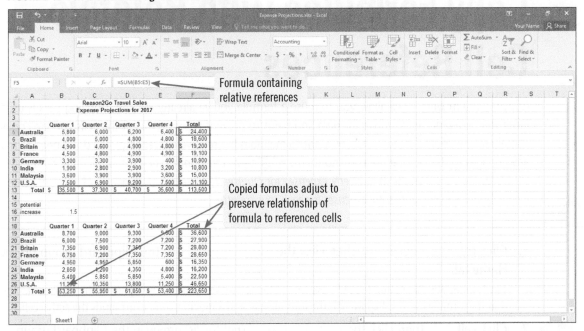

Formula containing relative references

Copied formulas adjust to preserve relationship of formula to referenced cells

FIGURE 2-13: Formulas containing absolute and relative references

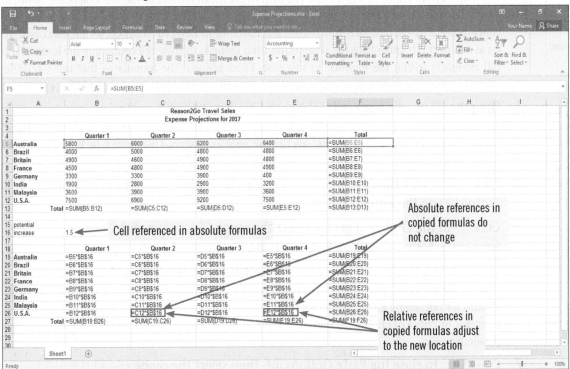

Absolute references in copied formulas do not change

Cell referenced in absolute formulas

Relative references in copied formulas adjust to the new location

Using a mixed reference

Sometimes when you copy a formula, you want to change the row reference, but keep the column reference the same. This type of cell referencing combines elements of both absolute and relative referencing and is called a **mixed reference**. For example, when copied, a formula containing the mixed reference C$14 would change the column letter relative to its new location, but not the row number. In the mixed reference $C14, the column letter would not change, but the row number would be updated relative to its location. Like an absolute reference, a mixed reference can be created by pressing the [F4] function key with the cell reference selected. With each press of the [F4] key, you cycle through all the possible combinations of relative, absolute, and mixed references (C14, $C$14, C$14, and $C14).

Copy Formulas with Relative Cell References

Learning Outcomes
• Copy and Paste formulas with relative cell references
• Examine Auto Fill and Paste Options
• Use the Fill button

Copying and moving a cell allow you to reuse a formula you've already created. Copying cells is usually faster than retyping the formulas in them and helps to prevent typing errors. If the cells you are copying contain relative cell references and you want to maintain the relative referencing, you don't need to make any changes to the cells before copying them. **CASE** ▶ *You want to copy the formula in cell B21, which calculates the 30% increase in quarterly expenses for Quarter 1, to cells C21 through E21. You also want to create formulas to calculate total expenses for each tour country.*

STEPS

1. **Click cell B21 if necessary, then click the Copy button 🖼 in the Clipboard group on the Home tab**

   The formula for calculating the 30% expense increase during Quarter 1 is copied to the Clipboard. Notice that the formula =B12*1.3 appears in the formula bar, and a moving border surrounds the active cell.

2. **Click cell C21, then click the Paste button 🖼 (not the list arrow) in the Clipboard group**

   The formula from cell B21 is copied into cell C21, where the new result of 45850.688 appears. Notice in the formula bar that the cell references have changed so that cell C12 is referenced instead of B12. This formula contains a relative cell reference, which tells Excel to substitute new cell references within the copied formulas as necessary. This maintains the same relationship between the new cell containing the formula and the cell references within the formula. In this case, Excel adjusted the formula so that cell C12—the cell reference nine rows above C21—replaced cell B12, the cell reference nine rows above B21.

3. **Drag the fill handle from cell C21 to cell E21**

   A formula similar to the one in cell C21 now appears in cells D21 and E21. After you use the fill handle to copy cell contents, the **Auto Fill Options button** appears, as shown in **FIGURE 2-14**. You can use the Auto Fill Options button to fill the cells with only specific elements of the copied cell if you wish.

4. **Click cell F4, click the AutoSum button Σ in the Editing group, then click the Enter button ✓ on the formula bar**

5. **Click 🖼 in the Clipboard group, select the range F5:F6, then click 🖼**

   See **FIGURE 2-15**. After you click the Paste button, the **Paste Options button** appears.

6. **Click the Paste Options button 🖼 (Ctrl) ▾ adjacent to the selected range**

   You can use the Paste options list to paste only specific elements of the copied selection if you wish. The formula for calculating total expenses for tours in Britain appears in the formula bar. You would like totals to appear in cells F7:F11. The Fill button in the Editing group can be used to copy the formula into the remaining cells.

7. **Press [Esc] to close the Paste Options list, then select the range F6:F11**

8. **Click the Fill button 🖼 in the Editing group, then click Down**

   The formulas containing relative references are copied to each cell. Compare your worksheet to **FIGURE 2-16**.

9. **Save your work**

FIGURE 2-14: Formula copied using the fill handle

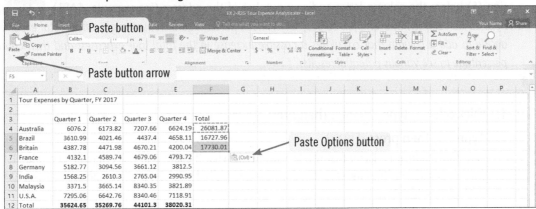

Auto Fill Options button

FIGURE 2-15: Formulas pasted in the range F5:F6

Paste button

Paste button arrow

Paste Options button

	Quarter 1	Quarter 2	Quarter 3	Quarter 4	Total
1 Tour Expenses by Quarter, FY 2017					
4 Australia	6076.2	6173.82	7207.66	6624.19	26081.87
5 Brazil	3610.99	4021.46	4437.4	4658.11	16727.96
6 Britain	4387.78	4471.98	4670.21	4200.04	17730.01
7 France	4132.1	4589.74	4679.06	4793.72	
8 Germany	5182.77	3094.56	3661.12	3812.5	
9 India	1568.25	2610.3	2765.04	2990.95	
10 Malaysia	3371.5	3665.14	8340.35	3821.89	
11 U.S.A.	7295.06	6642.76	8340.46	7118.91	
12 Total	35624.65	35269.76	44101.3	38020.31	

FIGURE 2-16: Formula copied using Fill Down

Fill button

=SUM(B6:E6)

Filled cells

	Quarter 1	Quarter 2	Quarter 3	Quarter 4	Total
1 Tour Expenses by Quarter, FY 2017					
4 Australia	6076.2	6173.82	7207.66	6624.19	26081.87
5 Brazil	3610.99	4021.46	4437.4	4658.11	16727.96
6 Britain	4387.78	4471.98	4670.21	4200.04	17730.01
7 France	4132.1	4589.74	4679.06	4793.72	18194.62
8 Germany	5182.77	3094.56	3661.12	3812.5	15750.95
9 India	1568.25	2610.3	2765.04	2990.95	9934.54
10 Malaysia	3371.5	3665.14	8340.35	3821.89	19198.88
11 U.S.A.	7295.06	6642.76	8340.46	7118.91	29397.19
12 Total	35624.65	35269.76	44101.3	38020.31	

Using Paste Preview

You can selectively copy formulas, values, or other choices using the Paste list arrow, and you can see how the pasted contents will look using the Paste Preview feature. When you click the Paste list arrow, a gallery of paste option icons opens. When you point to an icon, a preview of how the content will be pasted using that option is shown in the worksheet. Options include pasting values only, pasting values with number formatting, pasting formulas only, pasting formatting only, pasting transposed data so that column data appears in rows and row data appears in columns, and pasting with no borders (to remove any borders around pasted cells).

Copy Formulas with Absolute Cell References

Learning
Outcomes
• Create an absolute
  cell reference
• Use the fill handle
  to copy absolute
  cell references

When copying cells, you might want one or more cell references in a formula to remain unchanged. In such an instance, you need to apply an absolute cell reference before copying the formula to preserve the specific cell address when the formula is copied. You create an absolute reference by placing a dollar sign ($) before the column letter and row number of the address (for example, $A$1). **CASE** *You need to do some what-if analysis to see how various percentage increases might affect total expenses. You decide to add a column that calculates a possible increase in the total tour expenses, and then change the percentage to see various potential results.*

STEPS

1. **Click cell** G1, **type** Change, **then press** [Enter]

2. **Type** 1.1, **then press** [Enter]
   You store the increase factor that will be used in the what-if analysis in this cell (G2). The value 1.1 can be used to calculate a 10% increase: anything you multiply by 1.1 returns an amount that is 110% of the original amount.

3. **Click cell** H3, **type** What if?, **then press** [Enter]

4. **In cell** H4, **type** =, **click cell** F4, **type** *, **click cell** G2, **then click the** Enter button ☑ **on the formula bar**
   The result, 28690.1, appears in cell H4. This value represents the total annual expenses for Australia if there is a 10% increase. You want to perform a what-if analysis for all the tour countries.

QUICK TIP
Before you copy or move a formula, always check to see if you need to use an absolute cell reference.

5. **Drag the fill handle from cell** H4 **to cell** H11
   The resulting values in the range H5:H11 are all zeros, which is not the result you wanted. Because you used relative cell addressing in cell H4, the copied formula adjusted so that the formula in cell H5 is =F5*G3; because there is no value in cell G3, the result is 0, an error. You need to use an absolute reference in the formula to keep the formula from adjusting itself. That way, it will always reference cell G2.

QUICK TIP
When changing a cell reference to an absolute reference, make sure the reference is selected or the insertion point is next to it in the cell before pressing [F4].

6. **Click cell** H4, **press** [F2] **to change to Edit mode, then press** [F4]
   When you press [F2], the range finder outlines the arguments of the equation in blue and red. The insertion point appears next to the G2 cell reference in cell H4. When you press [F4], dollar signs are inserted in the G2 cell reference, making it an absolute reference. See **FIGURE 2-17**.

7. **Click** ☑, **then drag the** fill handle **from cell** H4 **to cell** H11
   Because the formula correctly contains an absolute cell reference, the correct values for a 10% increase appear in cells H4:H11. You now want to see what a 20% increase in expenses looks like.

8. **Click cell** G2, **type** 1.2, **then click** ☑
   The values in the range H4:H11 change to reflect the 20% increase. Compare your worksheet to **FIGURE 2-18**.

9. **Save your work**

FIGURE 2-17: Absolute reference created in formula

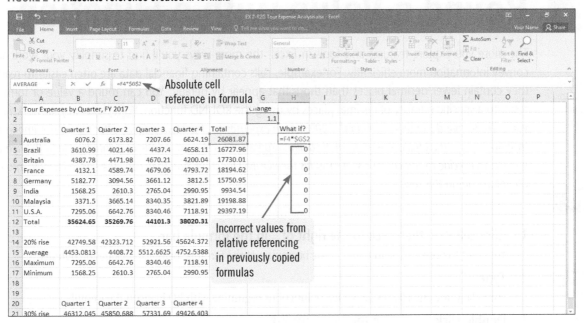

Absolute cell reference in formula → =F4*$G$2

Incorrect values from relative referencing in previously copied formulas

FIGURE 2-18: What-if analysis with modified change factor

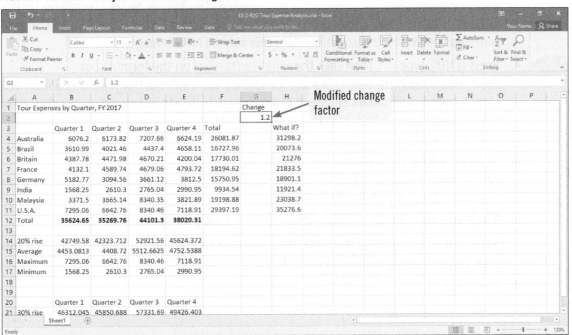

Modified change factor

Using the fill handle for sequential text or values

Often, you need to fill cells with sequential text: months of the year, days of the week, years, or text plus a number (Quarter 1, Quarter 2,...). For example, you might want to create a worksheet that calculates data for every month of the year. Using the fill handle, you can quickly and easily create labels for the months of the year just by typing "January" in a cell. Drag the fill handle from the cell containing "January" until you have all the monthly labels you need. You can also easily fill cells with a date sequence by dragging the fill handle on a single cell containing a date. You can

fill cells with a number sequence (such as 1, 2, 3,...) by dragging the fill handle on a selection of two or more cells that contain the sequence. To create a number sequence using the value in a single cell, press and hold [Ctrl] as you drag the fill handle of the cell. As you drag the fill handle, Excel automatically extends the existing sequence into the additional cells. (The content of the last filled cell appears in the ScreenTip.) To choose from all the fill series options for the current selection, click the Fill button in the Editing group on the Home tab, then click Series to open the Series dialog box.

Round a Value with a Function

Learning
Outcomes
• Use Formula
  AutoComplete to
  insert a function
• Copy an edited
  formula

The more you explore features and tools in Excel, the more ways you'll find to simplify your work and convey information more efficiently. For example, cells containing financial data are often easier to read if they contain fewer decimal places than those that appear by default. You can round a value or formula result to a specific number of decimal places by using the ROUND function. **CASE** ▶ *In your worksheet, you'd like to round the cells showing the 20% rise in expenses to show fewer digits; after all, it's not important to show cents in the projections, only whole dollars. You want Excel to round the calculated value to the nearest integer. You decide to edit cell B14 so it includes the ROUND function, and then copy the edited formula into the other formulas in this row.*

STEPS

1. **Click cell B14, then click to the right of = in the formula bar**

   You want to position the function at the beginning of the formula, before any values or arguments.

2. **Type RO**

   Formula AutoComplete displays a list of functions beginning with RO beneath the formula bar.

3. **Double-click ROUND in the functions list**

   The new function and an opening parenthesis are added to the formula, as shown in **FIGURE 2-19**. A few additional modifications are needed to complete your edit of the formula. You need to indicate the number of decimal places to which the function should round numbers, and you also need to add a closing parenthesis around the set of arguments that comes after the ROUND function.

4. **Press [END], type ,0), then click the Enter button ✓ on the formula bar**

   The comma separates the arguments within the formula, and 0 indicates that you don't want any decimal places to appear in the calculated value. When you complete the edit, the parentheses at either end of the formula briefly become bold, indicating that the formula has the correct number of open and closed parentheses and is balanced.

5. **Drag the fill handle from cell B14 to cell E14**

   The formula in cell B14 is copied to the range C14:E14. All the values are rounded to display no decimal places. Compare your worksheet to **FIGURE 2-20**.

6. **Scroll down so row 25 is visible, click cell A25, type your name, then click ✓**

7. **Save your work, preview the worksheet in the Print place in Backstage view, then submit your work to your Instructor as directed**

8. **Exit Excel**

Using Auto Fill options

When you use the fill handle to copy cells, the Auto Fill Options button appears. Auto Fill options differ depending on what you are copying. If you had selected cells containing a series (such as "Monday" and "Tuesday") and then used the fill handle, you would see options for continuing the series (such as "Wednesday" and "Thursday") or for simply pasting the copied cells. Clicking the Auto Fill Options button opens a list that lets you choose from the following options: Copy Cells, Fill Series (if applicable), Fill Formatting Only, Fill Without Formatting, or Flash Fill. Choosing Copy Cells means that the cell's contents and its formatting will be copied. The Fill Formatting Only option copies only the formatting attributes, but not cell contents. The Fill Without Formatting option copies the cell contents, but no formatting attributes. Copy Cells is the default option when using the fill handle to copy a cell, so if you want to copy the cell's contents and its formatting, you can ignore the Auto Fill Options button. The Flash Fill option allows you to create customized fill ranges on the fly, such as 2, 4, 6, 8, 10, by entering at least two values in a pattern: Excel automatically senses the pattern.

FIGURE 2-19: **ROUND function added to an existing formula**

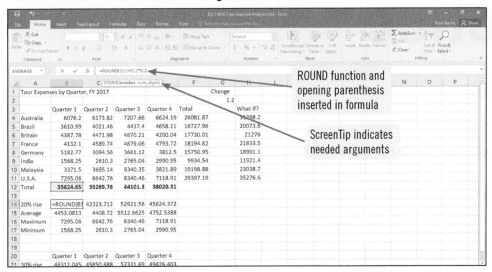

ROUND function and opening parenthesis inserted in formula

ScreenTip indicates needed arguments

FIGURE 2-20: **Completed worksheet**

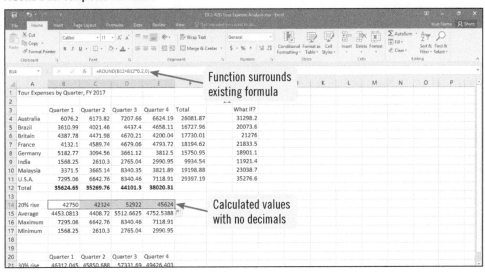

Function surrounds existing formula

Calculated values with no decimals

Excel 2016

Creating a new workbook using a template

Excel **templates** are predesigned workbook files intended to save time when you create common documents such as balance sheets, budgets, or time cards. Templates contain labels, values, formulas, and formatting, so all you have to do is customize them with your own information. Excel comes with many templates, and you can also create your own or find additional templates on the web. Unlike a typical workbook, which has the file extension .xlsx, a template has the extension .xltx. To create a workbook using a template, click the File tab, then click New on the navigation bar. The New place in Backstage view displays thumbnails of some of the many templates available. The Blank workbook template is selected by default and is used to create a blank workbook with no content or special formatting. To select a different template, click one of the selections in the New place, view the preview, then click Create. FIGURE 2-21 shows an example. (Your available templates may differ.) When you click

Create, a new workbook is created based on the template; when you save the new file in the default format, it has the regular .xlsx extension. To save a workbook of your own as a template, open the Save As dialog box, click the Save as type list arrow, then change the file type to Excel Template.

FIGURE 2-21: **Previewing the Budget Planner template**

Practice

Concepts Review

Label each element of the Excel worksheet window shown in FIGURE 2-22.

FIGURE 2-22

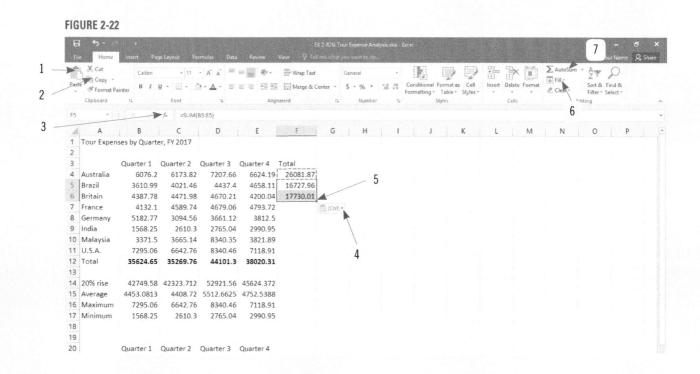

Match each term or button with the statement that best describes it.

8. Launcher
9. Fill handle
10. Drag-and-drop method
11. Formula AutoComplete
12. [Delete] key

a. Clears the contents of selected cells
b. Item on the Ribbon that opens a dialog box or task pane
c. Lets you move or copy data from one cell to another without using the Clipboard
d. Displays an alphabetical list of functions from which you can choose
e. Lets you copy cell contents or continue a series of data into a range of selected cells

Working with Formulas and Functions

Select the best answer from the list of choices.

13. **You can use any of the following features to enter a new function except:**
    - **a.** Insert Function button.
    - **b.** Formula AutoComplete.
    - **c.** AutoSum list arrow.
    - **d.** Clipboard.

14. **Which key do you press and hold to copy while dragging and dropping selected cells?**
    - **a.** [Alt]
    - **b.** [Ctrl]
    - **c.** [F2]
    - **d.** [Tab]

15. **What type of cell reference is C$19?**
    - **a.** Relative
    - **b.** Absolute
    - **c.** Mixed
    - **d.** Certain

16. **Which key do you press to convert a relative cell reference to an absolute cell reference?**
    - **a.** [F2]
    - **b.** [F4]
    - **c.** [F5]
    - **d.** [F6]

17. **What type of cell reference changes when it is copied?**
    - **a.** Circular
    - **b.** Absolute
    - **c.** Relative
    - **d.** Specified

Skills Review

1. **Create a complex formula.**
   - **a.** Open EX 2-2.xlsx from the location where you store your Data Files, then save it as **EX 2-Construction Supply Company Inventory**.
   - **b.** Select the range B4:B8, click the Totals tab in the Quick Analysis tool, then click the AutoSum button.
   - **c.** Use the fill handle to copy the formula in cell B9 to cells C9:E9.
   - **d.** In cell B11, create a complex formula that calculates a 30% decrease in the total number of cases of pylons.
   - **e.** Use the fill handle to copy this formula into cell C11 through cell E11.
   - **f.** Save your work.

2. **Insert a function.**
   - **a.** Use the AutoSum list arrow to create a formula in cell B13 that averages the number of cases of pylons in each storage area.
   - **b.** Use the Insert Function button to create a formula in cell B14 that calculates the maximum number of cases of pylons in a storage area.
   - **c.** Use the AutoSum list arrow to create a formula in cell B15 that calculates the minimum number of cases of pylons in a storage area.
   - **d.** Save your work.

3. Type a function.

   a. In cell C13, type a formula that includes a function to average the number of cases of bricks in each storage area. (*Hint*: Use Formula AutoComplete to enter the function.)

   b. In cell C14, type a formula that includes a function to calculate the maximum number of cases of bricks in a storage area.

   c. In cell C15, type a formula that includes a function to calculate the minimum number of cases of bricks in a storage area.

   d. Save your work.

4. Copy and move cell entries.

   a. Select the range B3:F3.

   b. Copy the selection to the Clipboard.

   c. Open the Clipboard task pane, then paste the selection into cell B17.

   d. Close the Clipboard task pane, then select the range A4:A9.

   e. Use the drag-and-drop method to copy the selection to cell A18. (*Hint*: The results should fill the range A18:A23.)

   f. Save your work.

5. Understand relative and absolute cell references.

   a. Write a brief description of the difference between relative and absolute references.

   b. List at least three situations in which you think a business might use an absolute reference in its calculations. Examples can include calculations for different types of worksheets, such as time cards, invoices, and budgets.

6. Copy formulas with relative cell references.

   a. Calculate the total in cell F4.

   b. Use the Fill button to copy the formula in cell F4 down to cells F5:F8.

   c. Select the range C13:C15.

   d. Use the fill handle to copy these cells to the range D13:F15.

   e. Save your work.

7. Copy formulas with absolute cell references.

   a. In cell H1, change the existing value to **1.575**.

   b. In cell H4, create a formula that multiplies F4 and an absolute reference to cell H1.

   c. Use the fill handle to copy the formula in cell H4 to cells H5 and H6.

   d. Use the Copy and Paste buttons to copy the formula in cell H4 to cells H7 and H8.

   e. Change the amount in cell H1 to **2.5**.

   f. Save your work.

Skills Review (continued)

8. Round a value with a function.

    a. Click cell H4.

    b. Edit this formula to include the ROUND function showing zero decimal places.

    c. Use the fill handle to copy the formula in cell H4 to the range H5:H8.

    d. Enter your name in cell A25, then compare your work to **FIGURE 2-23**.

    e. Save your work, preview the worksheet in Backstage view, then submit your work to your instructor as directed.

    f. Close the workbook, then exit Excel.

FIGURE 2-23

Independent Challenge 1

You are thinking of starting a small coffee shop where locals can gather. Before you begin, you need to evaluate what you think your monthly expenses will be. You've started a workbook, but need to complete the entries and add formulas.

a. Open EX 2-3.xlsx from the location where you store your Data Files, then save it as **EX 2-Coffee Shop Expenses**.

b. Make up your own expense data, and enter it in cells B4:B10. (Monthly sales are already included in the worksheet.)

c. Create a formula in cell C4 that calculates the annual rent.

d. Copy the formula in cell C4 to the range C5:C10.

e. Move the label in cell A15 to cell A14.

f. Create formulas in cells B11 and C11 that total the monthly and annual expenses.

g. Create a formula in cell C13 that calculates annual sales.

h. Create a formula in cell B14 that determines whether you will make a profit or loss, then copy the formula into cell C14.

i. Copy the labels in cells B3:C3 to cells E3:F3.

j. Type **Projected Increase** in cell G1, then type **.2** in cell H2.

k. Create a formula in cell E4 that calculates an increase in the monthly rent by the amount in cell H2. You will be copying this formula to other cells, so you'll need to use an absolute reference.

l. Create a formula in cell F4 that calculates the increased annual rent expense based on the calculation in cell E4.

m. Copy the formulas in cells E4:F4 into cells E5:F10 to calculate the remaining monthly and annual expenses.

n. Create a formula in cell E11 that calculates the total monthly expenses, then copy that formula to cell F11.

o. Copy the contents of cells B13:C13 into cells E13:F13.

p. Create formulas in cells E14 and F14 that calculate profit/loss based on the projected increase in monthly and annual expenses.

q. Change the projected increase to **.17**, then compare your work to the sample in **FIGURE 2-24**.

r. Enter your name in a cell in the worksheet.

s. Save your work, preview the worksheet in Backstage view, submit your work to your instructor as directed, close the workbook, and exit Excel.

FIGURE 2-24

	A	B	C	D	E	F	G	H	I
1	Estim	Your formulas go here (your formula results will differ)	nses				Projected Increase		
2								0.17	
3		Monthly	Annually		Monthly	Annually			
4	Rent	2500	30000		2925	35100			
5	Supplies	1600	19200		1872	22464			
6	Milk	3600	43200		4212	50544			
7	Sugar	1300	15600		1521	18252			
8	Pastries	850	10200		994.5	11934			
9	Coffee	600	7200		702	8424			
10	Utilities	750	9000		877.5	10530			
11	Total	**11200**	**134400**		13104	157248			
12									
13	Sales	24500	294000		23000	276000			
14	Profit/Loss	13300	159600		9896	118752			

Independent Challenge 2

The Office Specialists Center is a small, growing business that rents small companies space and provides limited business services. They have hired you to organize their accounting records using Excel. The owners want you to track the company's expenses. Before you were hired, one of the bookkeepers began entering last year's expenses in a workbook, but the analysis was never completed.

a. Start Excel, open EX 2-4.xlsx from the location where you store your Data Files, then save it as **EX 2-Office Specialists Center Finances**. The worksheet includes labels for functions such as the average, maximum, and minimum amounts of each of the expenses in the worksheet.

b. Think about what information would be important for the bookkeeping staff to know.

c. Using the Quick Analysis tool, create a formula in the Quarter 1 column that uses the SUM function, then copy that formula into the Total row for the remaining quarters.

d. Use the SUM function to create formulas for each expense in the Total column.

e. Create formulas for each expense and each quarter in the Average, Maximum, and Minimum columns and rows using the method of your choice.

f. Compare your worksheet to the sample shown in FIGURE 2-25.

g. Enter your name in cell A25, then save your work.

h. Preview the worksheet, then submit your work to your instructor as directed.

i. Close the workbook and exit Excel.

FIGURE 2-25

	A	B	C	D	E	F	G	H	I	J
1	Office Specialists Center									
2										
3	Operating Expenses for 2017									
4										
5	Expense	Quarter 1	Quarter 2	Quarter 3	Quarter 4	Total	Average	Maximum	Minimum	
6	Rent	10240	10240	10240	10240	40960	10240	10240	10240	
7	Utilities	9500	8482	7929	8596	34507	8626.75	9500	7929	
8	Payroll	24456	27922	26876	30415	109669	27417.3	30415	24456	
9	Insurance	9000	8594	8472	8523	34589	8647.25	9000	8472	
10	Education	4000	4081	7552	5006	20639	5159.75	7552	4000	
11	Inventory	15986	14115	14641	15465	60207	15051.8	15986	14115	
12	Total	73182	73434	75710	78245					
13										
14	Average	12197	12239	12618.3	13040.8		Your formulas go here			
15	Maximum	24456	27922	26876	30415					
16	Minimum	4000	4081	7552	5006					

Independent Challenge 3

As the accounting manager of a locally owned food co-op with multiple locations, it is your responsibility to calculate accrued sales tax payments on a monthly basis and then submit the payments to the state government. You've decided to use an Excel workbook to make these calculations.

a. Start Excel, then save a new, blank workbook to the drive and folder where you store your Data Files as **EX 2-Food Co-op Sales Tax Calculations**.

b. Decide on the layout for all columns and rows. The worksheet will contain data for six stores, which you can name by store number, neighborhood, or another method of your choice. For each store, you will calculate total sales tax based on the local sales tax rate. You'll also calculate total tax owed for all six locations.

c. Make up sales data for all six stores.

d. Enter the rate to be used to calculate the sales tax, using your own local rate.

e. Create formulas to calculate the sales tax owed for each location. If you don't know the local tax rate, use **6.5%**.

f. Create a formula to total all the accrued sales tax.

g. Use the ROUND function to eliminate any decimal places in the sales tax figures for each location and in the total due.

h. Add your name to the header, then compare your work to the sample shown in **FIGURE 2-26**.

i. Save your work, preview the worksheet, and submit your work to your instructor as directed.

j. Close the workbook and exit Excel.

FIGURE 2-26

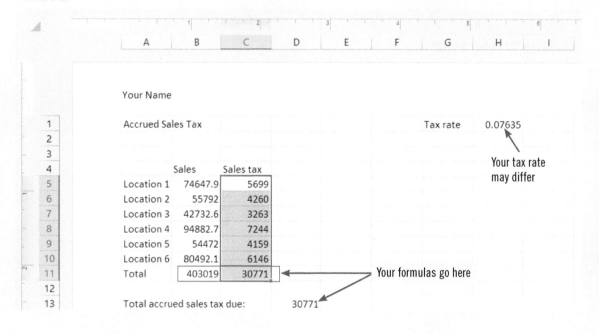

Independent Challenge 4: Explore

So many friends have come to you for help in understanding the various fees associated with purchasing a home that you've decided to create a business that specializes in helping first-time home-buyers. Your first task is to create a worksheet that clearly shows all the information a home buyer will need. Some fees are based on a percentage of the purchase price, and others are a flat fee; overall, they seem to represent a substantial amount above the purchase prices you see listed. A client has seen five houses so far that interest her; one is easily affordable, and the remaining four are all nice, but increasingly more expensive. You decide to create an Excel workbook to help her figure out the real cost of each home.

a. Find out the typical cost or percentage rate of at least three fees that are usually charged when buying a home and taking out a mortgage. (*Hint*: If you have access to the Internet, you can research the topic of home buying on the web, or you can ask friends about standard rates or percentages for items such as title insurance, credit reports, and inspection fees.)

b. Start Excel, then save a new, blank workbook to the location where you store your Data Files as **EX 2-Home Purchase Fees Worksheet**.

c. Create labels and enter data for at least five homes. If you enter this information across the columns in your worksheet, you should have one column for each house, with the purchase price in the cell below each label. Be sure to enter a different purchase price for each house.

d. Create labels for the Fees column and for an Amount or Rate column. Enter the information for each of the fees you have researched.

e. In each house column, enter formulas that calculate the fee for each item. The formulas (and use of absolute or relative referencing) will vary depending on whether the charges are a flat fee or based on a percentage of the purchase price. Make sure that the formulas for items that are based on a percentage of the purchase price (such as the fees for the Title Insurance Policy, Loan Origination, and Underwriter) contain absolute references. A sample of what your workbook might look like is shown in FIGURE 2-27.

f. Total the fees for each house, then create formulas that add the total fees to the purchase price.

g. Enter a title for the worksheet and include your client's name (or use Client 1) in the header.

h. Enter your name in the header, save your work, preview the worksheet, then submit your work to your instructor as directed.

i. Close the file and exit Excel.

FIGURE 2-27

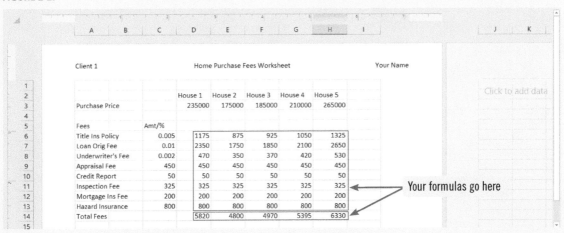

Visual Workshop

Create the worksheet shown in **FIGURE 2-28** using the skills you learned in this module. Save the workbook as **EX 2-Monthly Expenses** to the location where you store your Data Files. Enter your name and worksheet title in the header as shown, hide the gridlines, preview the worksheet, and then submit your work to your instructor as directed. (*Hint:* Change the Zoom factor to 90% by using the Zoom out button.)

FIGURE 2-28

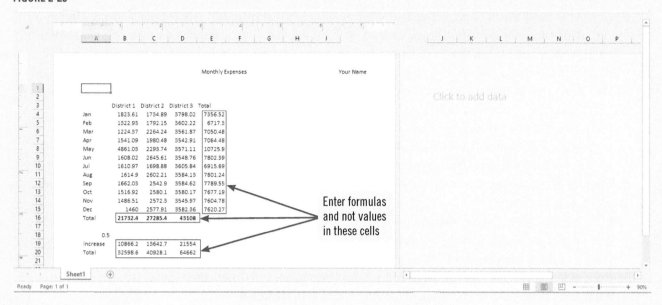

Formatting a Worksheet

CASE The marketing managers at Reason2Go have requested data from all R2G locations for advertising expenses incurred during the first quarter of this year. Mary Watson has created a worksheet listing this information. She asks you to format the worksheet to make it easier to read and to call attention to important data.

Module Objectives

After completing this module, you will be able to:

- Format values
- Change font and font size
- Change font styles and alignment
- Adjust column width
- Insert and delete rows and columns

- Apply colors, patterns, and borders
- Apply conditional formatting
- Rename and move a worksheet
- Check spelling

Files You Will Need

EX 3-1.xlsx   EX 3-4.xlsx
EX 3-2.xlsx   EX 3-5.xlsx
EX 3-3.xlsx

Format Values

The **format** of a cell determines how the labels and values look—for example, whether the contents appear boldfaced, italicized, or with dollar signs and commas. Formatting changes only the appearance of a value or label; it does not alter the actual data in any way. To format a cell or range, first you select it, then you apply the formatting using the Ribbon, Mini toolbar, or a keyboard shortcut. You can apply formatting before or after you enter data in a cell or range. **CASE** *Mary has provided you with a worksheet that details advertising expenses, and you're ready to improve its appearance and readability. You start by formatting some of the values so they are displayed as currency, percentages, and dates.*

STEPS

1. **Start Excel, open the file** EX 3-1.xlsx **from the location where you store your Data Files, then save it as** EX 3-R2G Advertising Expenses

   This worksheet is difficult to interpret because all the information is crowded and looks the same. In some columns, the contents appear cut off because there is too much data to fit given the current column width. You decide not to widen the columns yet, because the other changes you plan to make might affect column width and row height. The first thing you want to do is format the data showing the cost of each ad.

2. **Select the range** D4:D32, **then click the** Accounting Number Format button $ **in the Number group on the Home tab**

   The default Accounting **number format** adds dollar signs and two decimal places to the data, as shown in FIGURE 3-1. Formatting this data in Accounting format makes it clear that its values are monetary values. Excel automatically resizes the column to display the new formatting. The Accounting and Currency number formats are both used for monetary values, but the Accounting format aligns currency symbols and decimal points of numbers in a column.

3. **Select the range** F4:H32, **then click the** Comma Style button **in the Number group**

   The values in columns F, G, and H display the Comma Style format, which does not include a dollar sign but can be useful for some types of accounting data.

4. **Select the range** J4:J32, **click the** Number Format list arrow, **click** Percentage, **then click the** Increase Decimal button **in the Number group**

   The data in the % of Total column is now formatted with a percent sign (%) and three decimal places. The Number Format list arrow lets you choose from popular number formats and shows an example of what the selected cell or cells would look like in each format (when multiple cells are selected, the example is based on the first cell in the range). Each time you click the Increase Decimal button, you add one decimal place; clicking the button twice would add two decimal places.

5. **Click the** Decrease Decimal button **in the Number group** twice

   Two decimal places are removed from the percentage values in column J.

6. **Select the range** B4:B31, **then click the** launcher **in the Number group**

   The Format Cells dialog box opens with the Date category already selected on the Number tab.

7. **Select the first** 14-Mar-12 format **in the Type list box as shown in** FIGURE 3-2, **then click** OK

   The dates in column B appear in the 14-Mar-12 format. The second 14-Mar-12 format in the list (visible if you scroll down the list) displays all days in two digits (it adds a leading zero if the day is only a single-digit number), while the one you chose displays single-digit days without a leading zero.

8. **Select the range** C4:C31, **right-click the** range, **click** Format Cells **on the shortcut menu, click** 14-Mar **in the Type list box in the Format Cells dialog box, then click** OK

   Compare your worksheet to FIGURE 3-3.

9. **Press** [Ctrl][Home], **then save your work**

FIGURE 3-1: **Accounting number format applied to range**

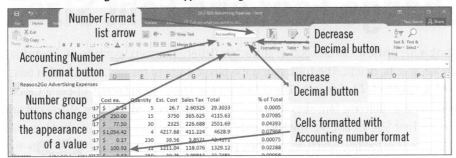

FIGURE 3-2: **Format Cells dialog box**

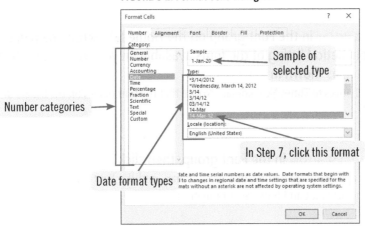

FIGURE 3-3: **Worksheet with formatted values**

Formatting as a table

Excel includes 60 predefined **table styles** to make it easy to format selected worksheet cells as a table. You can apply table styles to any range of cells that you want to format quickly, or even to an entire worksheet, but they're especially useful for those ranges with labels in the left column and top row, and totals in the bottom row or right column. To apply a table style, select the data to be formatted or click anywhere within the intended range (Excel can automatically detect a range of cells filled with data), click the Format as Table button in the Styles group on the Home tab, then click a style in the gallery, as shown in **FIGURE 3-4**. Table styles are organized in three categories: Light, Medium, and Dark. Once you click a style, Excel asks you to confirm the range selection, then applies the style. Once you have formatted a range as a table, you can use Live Preview to preview the table in other styles by pointing to any style in the Table Styles gallery.

FIGURE 3-4: **Table Styles gallery**

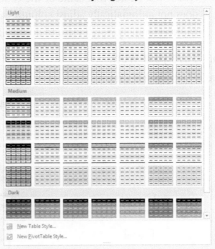

Change Font and Font Size

Learning
Outcomes
• Change a font
• Change a font size
• Use the Mini
toolbar

A **font** is the name for a collection of characters (letters, numbers, symbols, and punctuation marks) with a similar, specific design. The **font size** is the physical size of the text, measured in units called points. A **point** is equal to 1/72 of an inch. The default font and font size in Excel is 11-point Calibri. **TABLE 3-1** shows several fonts in different font sizes. You can change the font and font size of any cell or range using the Font and Font Size list arrows. The Font and Font Size list arrows appear on the Home tab on the Ribbon and on the Mini toolbar, which opens when you right-click a cell or range. **CASE** ▸ *You want to change the font and font size of the labels and the worksheet title so that they stand out more from the data.*

STEPS

1. **Click the** Font list arrow **in the Font group on the Home tab, scroll down in the Font list to see an alphabetical listing of the fonts available on your computer, then click** Times New Roman, **as shown in FIGURE 3-5**

   The font in cell A1 changes to Times New Roman. Notice that the font names on the list are displayed in the font they represent.

2. **Click the** Font Size list arrow **in the Font group, then click** 20

   The worksheet title appears in 20-point Times New Roman, and the Font and Font Size list boxes on the Home tab display the new font and font size information.

3. **Click the** Increase Font Size button A˘ **in the Font group twice**

   The font size of the title increases to 24 point.

4. **Select the range** A3:J3, **right-click, then click the** Font list arrow **on the Mini toolbar**

   The Mini toolbar includes the most commonly used formatting tools, so it's great for making quick formatting changes.

5. **Scroll down in the Font list and click** Times New Roman, **click the** Font Size list arrow **on the Mini toolbar, then click** 14

   The Mini toolbar closes when you move the pointer away from the selection. Compare your worksheet to **FIGURE 3-6**. Notice that some of the column labels are now too wide to appear fully in the column. Excel does not automatically adjust column widths to accommodate cell formatting; you have to adjust column widths manually. You'll learn to do this in a later lesson.

6. **Save your work**

TABLE 3-1: Examples of fonts and font sizes

font	12 point	24 point
Calibri	Excel	Excel
Playbill	Excel	Excel
Comic Sans MS	Excel	Excel
Times New Roman	Excel	Excel

FIGURE 3-5: Font list

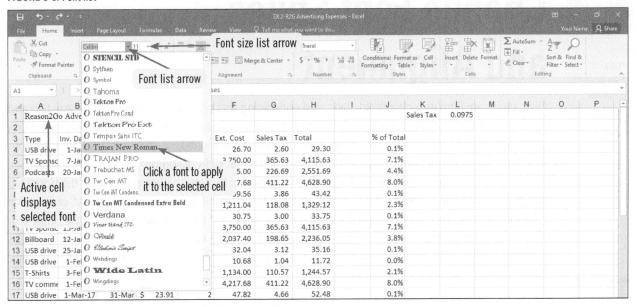

FIGURE 3-6: Worksheet with formatted title and column labels

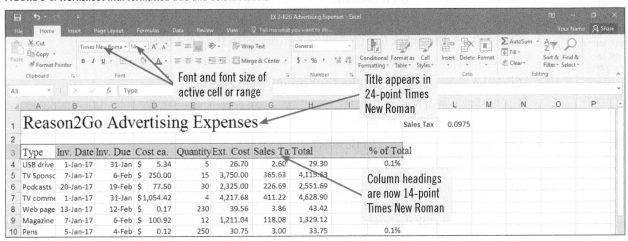

Inserting and adjusting online pictures and other images

You can illustrate your worksheets using online pictures and other images. Office.com makes many photos and animations available for your use. To add a picture to a worksheet, click the Online Pictures button in the Illustrations group on the Insert tab. The Insert Pictures window opens. Here you can search for online pictures (or Clip Art) from a variety of popular sources such as Facebook and Flickr, through the Bing search engine, or on OneDrive. To search, type one or more **keywords** (words related to your subject) in the appropriate Search text box, then press [Enter]. For example, pictures that relate to the keyword house in a search of Office.com appear in the Office.com window, as shown in **FIGURE 3-7**. When you double-click the image you want in the window, the image is inserted at the location of the active cell. To add images on your computer (or computers on your network) to a worksheet, click the Insert tab on the Ribbon, then click the Pictures button in the Illustrations group. Navigate to

the file you want, then click Insert. To resize an image, drag any corner sizing handle. To move an image, point inside the clip until the pointer changes to ⁺↖, then drag it to a new location.

FIGURE 3-7: Results of Online Picture search

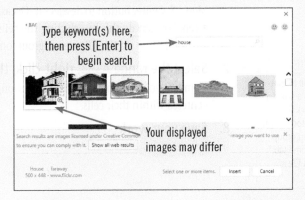

Learning
Outcomes
• Apply formatting
• Use the Format
  Painter
• Change cell
  alignment

Change Font Styles and Alignment

Font styles are formats such as bold, italic, and underlining that you can apply to affect the way text and numbers look in a worksheet. You can also change the **alignment** of labels and values in cells to position them in relation to the cells' edges—such as left-aligned, right-aligned, or centered. You can apply font styles and alignment options using the Home tab, the Format Cells dialog box, or the Mini toolbar. See **TABLE 3-2** for a description of common font style and alignment buttons that are available on the Home tab and the Mini toolbar. Once you have formatted a cell the way you want it, you can "paint" or copy the cell's formats into other cells by using the Format Painter button in the Clipboard group on the Home tab. This is similar to using copy and paste, but instead of copying cell contents, it copies only the cell's formatting. **CASE** *You want to further enhance the worksheet's appearance by adding bold and underline formatting and centering some of the labels.*

STEPS

QUICK TIP
You can use the following keyboard shortcuts to format a selected cell or range: [Ctrl][B] to bold, [Ctrl][I] to italicize, and [Ctrl][U] to underline.

1. **Press [Ctrl][Home], then click the Bold button B in the Font group on the Home tab**
   The title in cell A1 appears in bold.

2. **Click cell A3, then click the Underline button U in the Font group**
   The column label is now underlined.

3. **Click the Italic button I in the Font group, then click B**
   The heading now appears in boldface, underlined, italic type. Notice that the Bold, Italic, and Underline buttons in the Font group are all selected.

QUICK TIP
Overuse of any font style and random formatting can make a workbook difficult to read. Be consistent and add the same formatting to similar items throughout a worksheet or in related worksheets.

4. **Click the Italic button I to deselect it**
   The italic font style is removed from cell A3, but the bold and underline font styles remain.

5. **Click the Format Painter button in the Clipboard group, then select the range B3:J3**
   The formatting in cell A3 is copied to the rest of the column labels. To paint the formats on more than one selection, double-click the Format Painter button to keep it activated until you turn it off. You can turn off the Format Painter by pressing [Esc] or by clicking . You decide the title would look better if it were centered over the data columns.

6. **Select the range A1:H1, then click the Merge & Center button in the Alignment group**
   The Merge & Center button creates one cell out of the eight cells across the row, then centers the text in that newly created, merged cell. The title "Reason2Go Advertising Expenses" is centered across the eight columns you selected. To split a merged cell into its original components, select the merged cell, then click the Merge & Center button to deselect it. Occasionally, you may find that you want cell contents to wrap within a cell. You can do this by selecting the cells containing the text you want to wrap, then clicking the Wrap Text button in the Alignment group on the Home tab on the Ribbon.

QUICK TIP
To clear all formatting from a selected range, click the Clear button in the Editing group on the Home tab, then click Clear Formats.

7. **Select the range A3:J3, right-click, then click the Center button on the Mini toolbar**
   Compare your screen to **FIGURE 3-8**. Although they may be difficult to read, notice that all the headings are centered within their cells.

8. **Save your work**

FIGURE 3-8: Worksheet with font styles and alignment applied

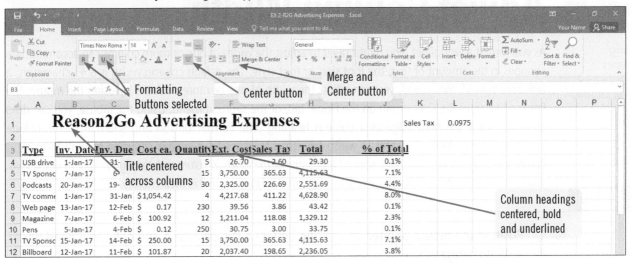

TABLE 3-2: Common font style and alignment buttons

button	description
B	Bolds text
I	Italicizes text
U	Underlines text
	Centers text across columns, and combines two or more selected, adjacent cells into one cell
	Aligns text at the left edge of the cell
	Centers text horizontally within the cell
	Aligns text at the right edge of the cell
	Wraps long text into multiple lines

Rotating and indenting cell entries

In addition to applying fonts and font styles, you can rotate or indent data within a cell to further change its appearance. You can rotate text within a cell by altering its alignment. Click the Home tab, select the cells you want to modify, then click the launcher in the Alignment group to open the Alignment tab of the Format Cells dialog box. Click a position in the Orientation box or type a number in the Degrees text box to rotate text from its default horizontal orientation, then click OK. You can indent cell contents using the Increase Indent button in the Alignment group, which moves cell contents to the right one space, or the Decrease Indent button, which moves cell contents to the left one space.

Adjust Column Width

As you format a worksheet, you might need to adjust the width of one or more columns to accommodate changes in the amount of text, the font size, or font style. The default column width is 8.43 characters, a little less than 1". With Excel, you can adjust the width of one or more columns by using the mouse, the Format button in the Cells group on the Home tab, or the shortcut menu. Using the mouse, you can drag or double-click the right edge of a column heading. The Format button and shortcut menu include commands for making more precise width adjustments. TABLE 3-3 describes common column formatting commands. **CASE** *You have noticed that some of the labels in columns A through J don't fit in the cells. You want to adjust the widths of the columns so that the labels appear in their entirety.*

STEPS

1. **Position the mouse pointer on the line between the column A and column B headings until it changes to ⟷**

   See FIGURE 3-9. The **column heading** is the box at the top of each column containing a letter. Before you can adjust column width using the mouse, you need to position the pointer on the right edge of the column heading for the column you want to adjust. The cell entry "TV commercials" is the widest in the column.

2. **Click and drag the ⟷ to the right until the column displays the "TV commercials" cell entries fully (approximately 15.29 characters, 1.23", or 112 pixels)**

   As you change the column width, a ScreenTip is displayed listing the column width. In Normal view, the ScreenTip lists the width in characters and pixels; in Page Layout view, the ScreenTip lists the width in inches and pixels.

3. **Position the pointer on the line between columns B and C until it changes to ⟷, then double-click**

   Double-clicking the right edge of a column heading activates the **AutoFit** feature, which automatically resizes the column to accommodate the widest entry in the column. Column B automatically widens to fit the widest entry, which is the column label "Inv. Date".

4. **Use AutoFit to resize columns C, D, and J**

5. **Select the range E5:H5**

   You can change the width of multiple columns at once, by first selecting either the column headings or at least one cell in each column.

6. **Click the Format button in the Cells group, then click Column Width**

   The Column Width dialog box opens. Column width measurement is based on the number of characters that will fit in the column when formatted in the Normal font and font size (in this case, 11-point Calibri).

7. **Drag the dialog box by its title bar if its placement obscures your view of the worksheet, type 11 in the Column width text box, then click OK**

   The widths of columns E, F, G, and H change to reflect the new setting. See FIGURE 3-10.

8. **Save your work**

TABLE 3-3: Common column formatting commands

command	description	available using
Column Width	Sets the width to a specific number of characters	Format button; shortcut menu
AutoFit Column Width	Fits to the widest entry in a column	Format button; mouse
Hide & Unhide	Hides or displays hidden column(s)	Format button; shortcut menu
Default Width	Resets column to worksheet's default column width	Format button

FIGURE 3-9: Preparing to change the column width

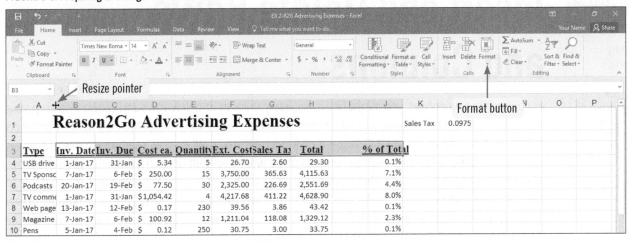

FIGURE 3-10: Worksheet with column widths adjusted

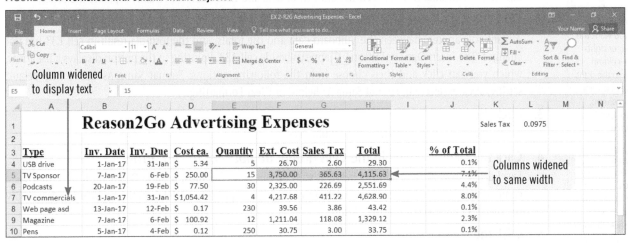

Changing row height

Changing row height is as easy as changing column width. Row height is calculated in points, the same units of measure used for fonts. The row height must exceed the size of the font you are using. Normally, you don't need to adjust row heights manually, because row heights adjust automatically to accommodate font size changes. If you format something in a row to be a larger point size, Excel adjusts the row to fit the largest point size in the row. However, you have just as many options for changing row height as you do column width. Using the mouse, you can place the ⬍ pointer on the line dividing a row heading from the heading below, and then drag to the desired height; double-clicking the line AutoFits the row height where necessary. You can also select one or more rows, then use the Row Height command on the shortcut menu, or click the Format button on the Home tab and click the Row Height or AutoFit Row Height command.

Insert and Delete Rows and Columns

Learning Outcomes
• Use the Insert dialog box
• Use column and row heading buttons to insert and delete

As you modify a worksheet, you might find it necessary to insert or delete rows and columns to keep your worksheet current. For example, you might need to insert rows to accommodate new inventory products or remove a column of yearly totals that are no longer necessary. When you insert a new row, the row is inserted above the cell pointer and the contents of the worksheet shift down from the newly inserted row. When you insert a new column, the column is inserted to the left of the cell pointer and the contents of the worksheet shift to the right of the new column. To insert multiple rows, select the same number of row headings as you want to insert before using the Insert command. **CASE** *You want to improve the overall appearance of the worksheet by inserting a row between the last row of data and the totals. Also, you have learned that row 27 and column J need to be deleted from the worksheet.*

STEPS

1. Right-click cell A32, then click Insert on the shortcut menu

The Insert dialog box opens. See **FIGURE 3-11**. You can choose to insert a column or a row; insert a single cell and shift the cells in the active column to the right; or insert a single cell and shift the cells in the active row down. An additional row between the last row of data and the totals will visually separate the totals.

2. Click the Entire row option button, then click OK

A blank row appears between the Billboard data and the totals, and the formula result in cell E33 has not changed. The Insert Options button [icon] appears beside cell A33. Pointing to the button displays a list arrow, which you can click and then choose from the following options: Format Same As Above (the default setting, already selected), Format Same As Below, or Clear Formatting.

3. Click the row 27 heading

All of row 27 is selected, as shown in **FIGURE 3-12**.

4. Click the Delete button in the Cells group; *do not click the list arrow*

Excel deletes row 27, and all rows below it shift up one row. You must use the Delete button or the Delete command on the shortcut menu to delete a row or column; pressing [Delete] on the keyboard removes only the *contents* of a selected row or column.

5. Click the column J heading

The percentage information is calculated elsewhere and is no longer necessary in this worksheet.

6. Click the Delete button in the Cells group

Excel deletes column J. The remaining columns to the right shift left one column.

7. Use AutoFit to resize columns F and H, then save your work

---

Hiding and unhiding columns and rows

When you don't want data in a column or row to be visible, but you don't want to delete it, you can hide the column or row. To hide a selected column, click the Format button in the Cells group on the Home tab, point to Hide & Unhide, then click Hide Columns. A hidden column is indicated by a dark green vertical line in its original position. This green line disappears when you click elsewhere in the worksheet. You can display a hidden column by selecting the columns on either side of the hidden column, clicking the Format button in the Cells group, pointing to Hide & Unhide, and then clicking Unhide Columns. (To hide or unhide one or more rows, substitute Hide Rows and Unhide Rows for the Hide Columns and Unhide Columns commands.)

FIGURE 3-11: Insert dialog box

Entire row
option button

FIGURE 3-12: **Worksheet with row 27 selected**

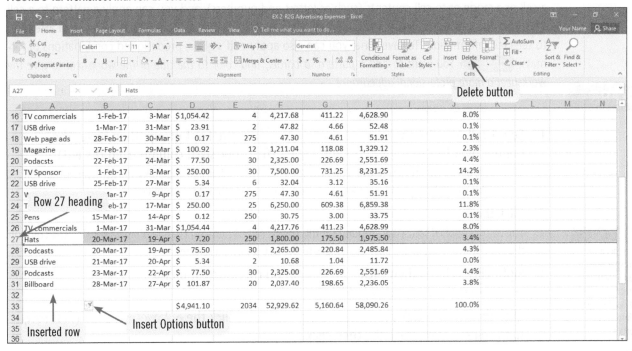

Delete button

Row 27 heading

Inserted row

Insert Options button

Adding and editing comments

Much of your work in Excel may be in collaboration with teammates with whom you share worksheets. You can share ideas with other worksheet users by adding comments within selected cells. To include a comment in a worksheet, click the cell where you want to place the comment, click the Review tab on the Ribbon, then click the New Comment button in the Comments group. You can type your comments in the resizable text box that opens containing the computer user's name. A small, red triangle appears in the upper-right corner of a cell containing a comment. If comments are not already displayed in a workbook, other users can point to the triangle to display the comment. To see all worksheet comments, as shown in **FIGURE 3-13**, click the Show All Comments button in the Comments group. To edit a comment, click the cell containing the comment, then click the Edit Comment button in the Comments

group. To delete a comment, click the cell containing the comment, then click the Delete button in the Comments group.

FIGURE 3-13: **Comments displayed in a worksheet**

	A	B	C	D
21	TV Sponsor	1-Feb-16	2-Mar	Food Network
22	Newspaper	25-Feb-16	26-Mar	Village Reader
23	Web page ads	10-Mar-16	9-Apr	Advertising Concepts
24	TV Sponsor	15-Feb-16	16-Mar	Food Network
25	Pens	15-Mar-16	14-Apr	Mass Appeal, Inc.
26	TV commercials	1-Mar-16	31-Mar	Discovery Channel
27	Podcasts	20-Mar-16	19-Apr	iPodAds
28	Newspaper	1-Apr-16	1-May	University Voice
29	Podcasts	10-Apr-16	10-May	iPodAds
30	Billboard	28-Mar-16	27-Apr	Advertising Concepts

Harriet McDonald:
I think this will turn out to be a very good decision.

Will Hoss:
Should we continue with this market, or expand to other types of publications?

Apply Colors, Patterns, and Borders

Learning
Outcomes
• Use Live Preview
  to apply color
  to cells
• Format cells using
  the shortcut menu
• Apply a border
  and pattern to
  a cell

You can use colors, patterns, and borders to enhance the overall appearance of a worksheet and make it easier to read. You can add these enhancements by using the Borders, Font Color, and Fill Color buttons in the Font group on the Home tab of the Ribbon and on the Mini toolbar, or by using the Fill tab and the Border tab in the Format Cells dialog box. You can open the Format Cells dialog box by clicking the dialog box launcher in the Font, Alignment, or Number group on the Home tab, or by right-clicking a selection, then clicking Format Cells on the shortcut menu. You can apply a color to the background of a cell or a range or to cell contents (such as letters and numbers), and you can apply a pattern to a cell or range. You can apply borders to all the cells in a worksheet or only to selected cells to call attention to selected information. To save time, you can also apply **cell styles**, predesigned combinations of formats. **CASE** ▸ *You want to add a pattern, a border, and color to the title of the worksheet to give the worksheet a more professional appearance.*

STEPS

1. **Select cell A1, click the** Fill Color list arrow 🎨 ▾ **in the Font group, then hover the pointer over the** Turquoise, Accent 2 color **(first row, sixth column from the left)**
   See **FIGURE 3-14**. Live Preview shows you how the color will look *before* you apply it. (Remember that cell A1 spans columns A through H because the Merge & Center command was applied.)

2. **Click the** Turquoise, Accent 2 color
   The color is applied to the background (or fill) of this cell. When you change fill or font color, the color on the Fill Color or Font Color button changes to the last color you selected.

3. **Right-click cell** A1, **then click** Format Cells **on the shortcut menu**
   The Format Cells dialog box opens.

4. **Click the** Fill tab, **click the** Pattern Style list arrow, **click the** 6.25% Gray style **(first row, sixth column from the left), then click** OK

5. **Click the** Borders list arrow ⊞ ▾ **in the Font group, then click** Thick Bottom Border
   Unlike underlining, which is a text-formatting tool, borders extend to the width of the cell, and can appear at the bottom of the cell, at the top, on either side, or on any combination of the four sides. It can be difficult to see a border when the cell is selected.

6. **Select the range** A3:H3, **click the** Font Color list arrow 🅰 **in the Font group, then click the** Blue, Accent 1 color **(first Theme Colors row, fifth column from the left) on the palette**
   The new color is applied to the labels in the selected range.

7. **Select the range** J1:K1, **click the** Cell Styles button **in the Styles group, click the** Neutral cell style **(first row, fourth column from the left) in the gallery, then AutoFit** column J
   The font and color change in the range, as shown in **FIGURE 3-15**.

8. **Save your work**

FIGURE 3-14: Live Preview of fill color

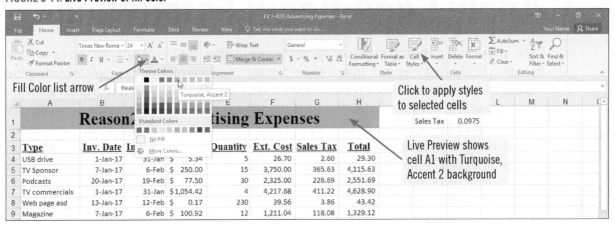

Fill Color list arrow

Click to apply styles to selected cells

Live Preview shows cell A1 with Turquoise, Accent 2 background

FIGURE 3-15: Worksheet with color, patterns, border, and style applied

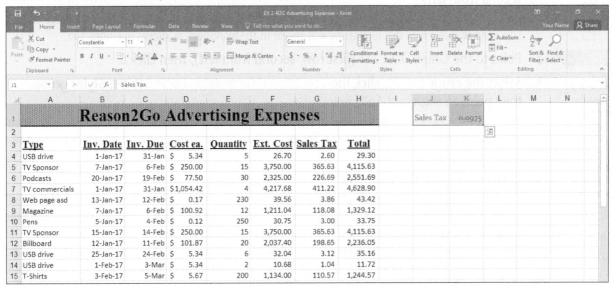

	A	B	C	D	E	F	G	H
1			Reason2Go Advertising Expenses					
2								
3	**Type**	**Inv. Date**	**Inv. Due**	**Cost ea.**	**Quantity**	**Ext. Cost**	**Sales Tax**	**Total**
4	USB drive	1-Jan-17	31-Jan	$ 5.34	5	26.70	2.60	29.30
5	TV Sponsor	7-Jan-17	6-Feb	$ 250.00	15	3,750.00	365.63	4,115.63
6	Podcasts	20-Jan-17	19-Feb	$ 77.50	30	2,325.00	226.69	2,551.69
7	TV commercials	1-Jan-17	31-Jan	$1,054.42	4	4,217.68	411.22	4,628.90
8	Web page asd	13-Jan-17	12-Feb	$ 0.17	230	39.56	3.86	43.42
9	Magazine	7-Jan-17	6-Feb	$ 100.92	12	1,211.04	118.08	1,329.12
10	Pens	5-Jan-17	4-Feb	$ 0.12	250	30.75	3.00	33.75
11	TV Sponsor	15-Jan-17	14-Feb	$ 250.00	15	3,750.00	365.63	4,115.63
12	Billboard	12-Jan-17	11-Feb	$ 101.87	20	2,037.40	198.65	2,236.05
13	USB drive	25-Jan-17	24-Feb	$ 5.34	6	32.04	3.12	35.16
14	USB drive	1-Feb-17	3-Mar	$ 5.34	2	10.68	1.04	11.72
15	T-Shirts	3-Feb-17	5-Mar	$ 5.67	200	1,134.00	110.57	1,244.57

Working with themes and cell styles

Using themes and cell styles makes it easier to ensure that your worksheets are consistent. A **theme** is a predefined set of formats that gives your Excel worksheet a professional look. Formatting choices included in a theme are colors, fonts, and line and fill effects. To apply a theme, click the Themes button in the Themes group on the Page Layout tab to open the Themes gallery, as shown in **FIGURE 3-16**, then click a theme in the gallery. **Cell styles** are automatically updated if you change a theme. For example, if you apply the 20% - Accent1 cell style to cell A1 in a worksheet that has no theme applied, the fill color changes to light blue with no pattern, and the font changes to Calibri. If you change the theme of the worksheet to Ion Boardroom, cell A1's fill color changes to red and the font changes to Century Gothic, because these are the new theme's associated formats.

FIGURE 3-16: Themes gallery

Apply Conditional Formatting

Learning
Outcomes
• Create conditional
  formatting in a
  range
• Change format-
  ting and parame-
  ters in conditional
  formatting

So far, you've used formatting to change the appearance of different types of data, but you can also use formatting to highlight important aspects of the data itself. For example, you can apply formatting that changes the font color to red for any cells where the value is greater than $100 and to green where the value is below $50. This is called **conditional formatting** because Excel automatically applies different formats to data if the data meets conditions you specify. The formatting is updated if you change data in the worksheet. You can also copy conditional formats the same way you copy other formats. **CASE** ▶ *Mary is concerned about advertising costs exceeding the yearly budget. You decide to use conditional formatting to highlight certain trends and patterns in the data so that it's easy to spot the most expensive advertising.*

STEPS

QUICK TIP
You can also use the
Quick Analysis tool
to create data bars,
but with fewer
choices.

1. **Select the range** H4:H30, **click the** Conditional Formatting button **in the Styles group on the Home tab, point to** Data Bars, **then point to the** Light Blue Data Bar **(second row, second from left)**

   Data bars are colored horizontal bars that visually illustrate differences between values in a range of cells. Live Preview shows how this formatting will appear in the worksheet, as shown in **FIGURE 3-17**.

QUICK TIP
You can apply an
Icon Set to a selected
range by clicking the
Conditional Format-
ting button in the
Styles group, then
pointing to Icon Sets;
icons appear within
the cells to illustrate
differences in values.

2. **Point to the** Green Data Bar **(first row, second from left), then click it**

3. **Select the range** F4:F30, **click the** Conditional Formatting button **in the Styles group, then point to** Highlight Cells Rules

   The Highlight Cells Rules submenu displays choices for creating different formatting conditions. For example, you can create a rule for values that are greater than or less than a certain amount, or between two amounts.

4. **Click** Between **on the submenu**

   The Between dialog box opens, displaying input boxes you can use to define the condition and a default format (Light Red Fill with Dark Red Text) selected for cells that meet that condition. Depending on the condition you select in the Highlight Cells Rules submenu (such as "Greater Than" or "Less Than"), this dialog box displays different input boxes. You define the condition using the input boxes and then assign the formatting you want to use for cells that meet that condition. Values used in input boxes for a condition can be constants, formulas, cell references, or dates.

QUICK TIP
To define custom for-
matting for data that
meets the condition,
click Custom Format
at the bottom of the
with list, and then
use the Format Cells
dialog box to set the
formatting to be
applied.

5. **Type** 2000 **in the first text box, type** 4000 **in the second text box, click the** with list arrow, **click** Light Red Fill, **compare your settings to** FIGURE 3-18, **then click** OK

   All cells with values between 2000 and 4000 in column F appear with a light red fill.

6. **Click cell** E7, **type** 3, **then press** [Enter]

   When the value in cell E7 changes, the formatting also changes because the new value meets the condition you set. Compare your results to **FIGURE 3-19**.

7. **Press** [Ctrl][Home] **to select cell A1, then save your work**

FIGURE 3-17: Previewing data bars in a range

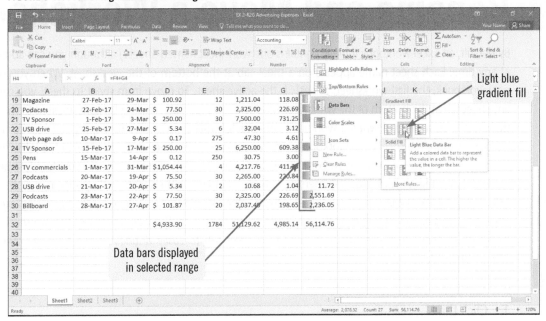

Data bars displayed
in selected range

Light blue
gradient fill

FIGURE 3-18: Between dialog box

Format for cells
meeting the condition

Input boxes

FIGURE 3-19: Worksheet with conditional formatting

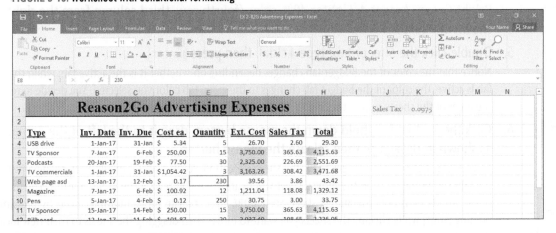

Managing conditional formatting rules

If you create a conditional formatting rule and then want to change a condition, you don't need to create a new rule; instead, you can modify the rule using the Rules Manager. Click the Conditional Formatting button in the Styles group, then click Manage Rules. The Conditional Formatting Rules Manager dialog box opens. Select the rule you want to edit, click Edit Rule, and then modify the settings in the Edit the Rule Description area in the Edit Formatting Rule dialog box. To change the formatting for a rule, click the Format Style button in the Edit the Rule Description area, select the formatting styles you want the text to have, then click OK three times to close the Format Cells dialog box, the Edit Formatting Rule dialog box, and the Conditional Formatting Rules Manager dialog box. The rule is modified, and the new conditional formatting is applied to the selected cells. To delete a rule, select the rule in the Conditional Formatting Rules Manager dialog box, then click the Delete Rule button.

Excel 2016

Rename and Move a Worksheet

Learning
Outcomes
• Rename a sheet
• Apply color to a
  sheet tab
• Reorder sheets in
  a workbook

By default, an Excel workbook initially contains one worksheet named Sheet1, although you can add sheets at any time. Each sheet name appears on a sheet tab at the bottom of the worksheet. When you open a new workbook, the first worksheet, Sheet1, is the active sheet. To move from sheet to sheet, you can click any sheet tab at the bottom of the worksheet window. The sheet tab scrolling buttons, located to the left of the sheet tabs, are useful when a workbook contains too many sheet tabs to display at once. To make it easier to identify the sheets in a workbook, you can rename each sheet and add color to the tabs. You can also organize them in a logical way. For instance, to better track performance goals, you could name each workbook sheet for an individual salesperson, and you could move the sheets so they appear in alphabetical order. **CASE** *In the current worksheet, Sheet1 contains information about actual advertising expenses. Sheet2 contains an advertising budget, and Sheet3 contains no data. You want to rename the two sheets in the workbook to reflect their contents, add color to a sheet tab to easily distinguish one from the other, and change their order.*

STEPS

1. **Click the Sheet2 tab**

   Sheet2 becomes active, appearing in front of the Sheet1 tab; this is the worksheet that contains the budgeted advertising expenses. See **FIGURE 3-20**.

2. **Click the Sheet1 tab**

   Sheet1, which contains the actual advertising expenses, becomes active again.

3. **Double-click the Sheet2 tab, type Budget, then press [Enter]**

   The new name for Sheet2 automatically replaces the default name on the tab. Worksheet names can have up to 31 characters, including spaces and punctuation.

4. **Right-click the Budget tab, point to Tab Color on the shortcut menu, then click the Bright Green, Accent 4, Lighter 40% color (fourth row, third column from the right) as shown in FIGURE 3-21**

5. **Double-click the Sheet1 tab, type Actual, then press [Enter]**

   Notice that the color of the Budget tab changes depending on whether it is the active tab; when the Actual tab is active, the color of the Budget tab changes to the green tab color you selected. You decide to rearrange the order of the sheets so that the Budget tab is to the left of the Actual tab.

6. **Click the Budget tab, hold down the mouse button, drag it to the left of the Actual tab, as shown in FIGURE 3-22, then release the mouse button**

   As you drag, the pointer changes to ▯, the sheet relocation pointer, and a small, black triangle just above the tabs shows the position the moved sheet will be in when you release the mouse button. The first sheet in the workbook is now the Budget sheet. See **FIGURE 3-23**. You can move multiple sheets by pressing and holding [Shift] while clicking the sheets you want to move, then dragging the sheets to their new location.

7. **Click the Actual sheet tab, click the Page Layout button ▤ on the status bar to open Page Layout view, enter your name in the left header text box, then click anywhere in the worksheet to deselect the header**

8. **Click the Page Layout tab on the Ribbon, click the Orientation button in the Page Setup group, then click Landscape**

9. **Right-click the Sheet3 tab, click Delete on the shortcut menu, press [Ctrl][Home], then save your work**

FIGURE 3-20: Sheet tabs in workbook

Sheet1 tab   Sheet2 tab

FIGURE 3-21: Tab Color palette

Sheet2 renamed

FIGURE 3-22: Moving the Budget sheet

Sheet relocation pointer

FIGURE 3-23: Reordered sheets

Budget sheet comes
before Actual sheet

Excel 2016

Copying, adding, and deleting worksheets

There are times when you may want to copy a worksheet. For example, a workbook might contain a sheet with Quarter 1 expenses, and you want to use that sheet as the basis for a sheet containing Quarter 2 expenses. To copy a sheet within the same workbook, press and hold [Ctrl], drag the sheet tab to the desired tab location, release the mouse button, then release [Ctrl]. A duplicate sheet appears with the same name as the copied sheet followed by "(2)" indicating that it is a copy. You can then rename the sheet to a more meaningful name. To copy a sheet to a different workbook, both the source and destination workbooks must be open. Select the sheet to copy or move, right-click the sheet tab, then click Move or Copy in the shortcut menu. Complete the information in the Move or Copy dialog box. Be sure to click the Create a copy check box if you are copying rather than moving the worksheet. Carefully check your calculation results whenever you move or copy a worksheet. You can add multiple worksheets to a workbook by clicking the Home tab on the Ribbon, pressing and holding [Shift], then clicking the number of existing worksheet tabs that correspond with the number of sheets you want to add, clicking the Insert list arrow in the Cells group on the Home tab, then clicking Insert Sheet. You can delete multiple worksheets from a workbook by clicking the Home tab, pressing and holding [Shift], clicking the sheet tabs of the worksheets you want to delete, clicking the Delete list arrow in the Cells group on the Home tab, then clicking Delete Sheet.

Check Spelling

Learning
Outcomes
• Describe how spell
  checking works
• Change the
  spelling using
  a suggestion
• Replace a word
  using Find & Select

Excel includes a spell checker to help you ensure that the words in your worksheet are spelled correctly. The spell checker scans your worksheet, displays words it doesn't find in its built-in dictionary, and suggests replacements when they are available. To check all of the sheets in a multiple-sheet workbook, you need to display each sheet individually and run the spell checker for each one. Because the built-in dictionary cannot possibly include all the words that anyone needs, you can add words to the dictionary, such as your company name, an acronym, or an unusual technical term. Once you add a word or term, the spell checker no longer considers that word misspelled. Any words you've added to the dictionary using Word, Access, or PowerPoint are also available in Excel. **CASE** *Before you distribute this workbook to Mary, you check the spelling.*

STEPS

QUICK TIP
The Spelling dialog box lists the name of the language currently being used in its title bar.

1. **Click the Review tab on the Ribbon, then click the Spelling button in the Proofing group**
   The Spelling: English (United States) dialog box opens, as shown in **FIGURE 3-24**, with "asd" selected as the first misspelled word in the worksheet, and with "ads" selected in the Suggestions list as a possible replacement. For any word, you have the option to Ignore this case of the flagged word, Ignore All cases of the flagged word, Change the word to the selected suggestion, Change All instances of the flagged word to the selected suggestion, or add the flagged word to the dictionary using Add to Dictionary.

2. **Click Change**
   Next, the spell checker finds the word "Podacsts" and suggests "Podcasts" as an alternative.

3. **Verify that the word Podcasts is selected in the Suggestions list, then click Change**
   When no more incorrect words are found, Excel displays a message indicating that the spell check is complete.

4. **Click OK**

5. **Click the Home tab, click Find & Select in the Editing group, then click Replace**
   The Find and Replace dialog box opens. You can use this dialog box to replace a word or phrase. It might be a misspelling of a proper name that the spell checker didn't recognize as misspelled, or it could simply be a term that you want to change throughout the worksheet. Mary has just told you that each instance of "Billboard" in the worksheet should be changed to "Sign."

6. **Type Billboard in the Find what text box, press [Tab], then type Sign in the Replace with text box**
   Compare your dialog box to **FIGURE 3-25**.

7. **Click Replace All, click OK to close the Microsoft Excel dialog box, then click Close to close the Find and Replace dialog box**
   Excel has made two replacements.

8. **Click the File tab, click Print on the navigation bar, click the No Scaling setting in the Settings section on the Print tab, then click Fit Sheet on One Page**

9. **Click the Return button ⬅ to return to your worksheet, save your work, submit it to your instructor as directed, close the workbook, then exit Excel**
   The completed worksheet is shown in **FIGURE 3-26**.

Emailing a workbook

You can send an entire workbook from within Excel using your installed email program, such as Microsoft Outlook. To send a workbook as an email message attachment, open the workbook, click the File tab, then click Share on the navigation bar. With the Email option selected in the Share section in Backstage view, click Send as Attachment in the right pane. An email message opens in your default email program with the workbook automatically attached; the filename appears in the Attached field. Complete the To and optional Cc fields, include a message if you wish, then click Send.

FIGURE 3-24: Spelling: English (United States) dialog box

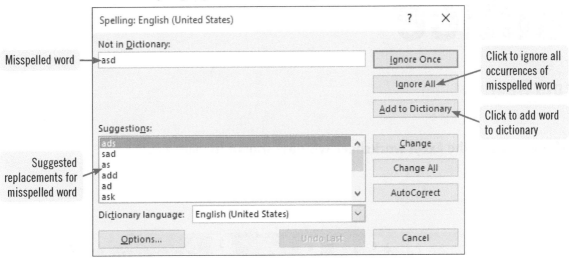

Misspelled word → [Not in Dictionary: asd]

Click to ignore all occurrences of misspelled word

Click to add word to dictionary

Suggested replacements for misspelled word → [Suggestions: ads, sad, as, add, ad, ask]

FIGURE 3-25: Find and Replace dialog box

Find and Replace

Find | Replace

Find what: Billboard

Replace with: Sign

Options >>

Replace All | Replace | Find All | Find Next | Close

FIGURE 3-26: Completed worksheet

Your Name

Reason2Go Advertising Expenses

Sales Tax   0.0975

Type	Inv. Date	Inv. Due	Cost ea.	Quantity	Ext. Cost	Sales Tax	Total
USB drive	1-Jan-17	31-Jan	$ 5.34	5	26.70	2.60	29.30
TV Sponsor	7-Jan-17	6-Feb	$ 250.00	15	3,750.00	365.63	4,115.63
Podcasts	20-Jan-17	19-Feb	$ 77.50	30	2,325.00	226.69	2,551.69
TV commercials	1-Jan-17	31-Jan	$ 1,054.42	3	3,163.26	308.42	3,471.68
Web page ads	13-Jan-17	12-Feb	$ 0.17	230	39.56	3.86	43.42
Magazine	7-Jan-17	6-Feb	$ 100.92	12	1,211.04	118.08	1,329.12
Pens	5-Jan-17	4-Feb	$ 0.12	250	30.75	3.00	33.75
TV Sponsor	15-Jan-17	14-Feb	$ 250.00	15	3,750.00	365.63	4,115.63
Sign	12-Jan-17	11-Feb	$ 101.87	20	2,037.40	198.65	2,236.05
USB drive	25-Jan-17	24-Feb	$ 5.34	6	32.04	3.12	35.16
USB drive	1-Feb-17	3-Mar	$ 5.34	2	10.68	1.04	11.72
T-Shirts	3-Feb-17	5-Mar	$ 5.67	200	1,134.00	110.57	1,244.57
TV commercials	1-Feb-17	3-Mar	$ 1,054.42	4	4,217.68	411.22	4,628.90
USB drive	1-Mar-17	31-Mar	$ 23.91	2	47.82	4.66	52.48
Web page ads	28-Feb-17	30-Mar	$ 0.17	275	47.30	4.61	51.91
Magazine	27-Feb-17	29-Mar	$ 100.92	12	1,211.04	118.08	1,329.12
Podcasts	22-Feb-17	24-Mar	$ 77.50	30	2,325.00	226.69	2,551.69
TV Sponsor	1-Feb-17	3-Mar	$ 250.00	30	7,500.00	731.25	8,231.25
USB drive	25-Feb-17	27-Mar	$ 5.34	6	32.04	3.12	35.16
Web page ads	10-Mar-17	9-Apr	$ 0.17	275	47.30	4.61	51.91
TV Sponsor	15-Feb-17	17-Mar	$ 250.00	25	6,250.00	609.38	6,859.38
Pens	15-Mar-17	14-Apr	$ 0.12	250	30.75	3.00	33.75
TV commercials	1-Mar-17	31-Mar	$ 1,054.44	4	4,217.76	411.23	4,628.99
Podcasts	20-Mar-17	19-Apr	$ 75.50	30	2,265.00	220.84	2,485.84
USB drive	21-Mar-17	20-Apr	$ 5.34	2	10.68	1.04	11.72
Podcasts	23-Mar-17	22-Apr	$ 77.50	30	2,325.00	226.69	2,551.69
Sign	28-Mar-17	27-Apr	$ 101.87	20	2,037.40	198.65	2,236.05
			$ 4,933.90	1783	50,075.20	4,882.33	54,957.53

Practice

Concepts Review

Label each element of the Excel worksheet window shown in FIGURE 3-27.

FIGURE 3-27

Match each command or button with the statement that best describes it.

8. Spelling button
9. $
10. 🖌 ·
11. [Ctrl][Home]
12. 🔲
13. Conditional formatting

a. Checks for apparent misspellings in a worksheet
b. Adds dollar signs and two decimal places to selected data
c. Displays fill color options for a cell
d. Moves cell pointer to cell A1
e. Centers cell contents across multiple cells
f. Changes formatting of a cell that meets a certain rule

Select the best answer from the list of choices.

14. **Which of the following is an example of Accounting number format?**

    a. 5555

    c. 55.55%

    b. $5,555.55

    d. 5,555.55

15. **What is the name of the feature used to resize a column to accommodate its widest entry?**

    a. AutoFormat

    c. AutoResize

    b. AutoFit

    d. AutoRefit

16. **Which button copies multiple formats from selected cells to other cells?**

    a. [↺]

    c. [A⌃]

    b. [⌐]

    d. [🖌]

17. **Which button increases the number of decimal places in selected cells?**

    a. [←.0 .00]

    c. [⇥≣]

    b. [.00 →.0]

    d. [⇤≣]

18. **Which button removes the italic font style from selected cells?**

    a. [*I*]

    c. [*I*]

    b. [B]

    d. [U]

19. **What feature is used to delete a conditional formatting rule?**

    a. Rules Reminder

    c. Condition Manager

    b. Conditional Formatting Rules Manager

    d. Format Manager

Skills Review

1. **Format values.**

    a. Start Excel, open the file EX 3-2.xlsx from the location where you store your Data Files, then save it as **EX 3-Health Insurance Premiums**.

    b. Use the Sum function to enter a formula in cell B10 that totals the number of employees.

    c. Create a formula in cell C5 that calculates the monthly insurance premium for the accounting department. (*Hint*: Make sure you use the correct type of cell reference in the formula. To calculate the department's monthly premium, multiply the number of employees by the monthly premium in cell B14.)

    d. Copy the formula in cell C5 to the range C6:C10.

    e. Format the range C5:C10 using Accounting number format.

    f. Change the format of the range C6:C9 to the Comma Style.

    g. Reduce the number of decimals in cell B14 to 0 using a button in the Number group on the Home tab.

    h. Save your work.

2. **Change font and font sizes.**

    a. Select the range of cells containing the column labels (in row 4).

    b. Change the font of the selection to Times New Roman.

    c. Increase the font size of the selection to 12 points.

    d. Increase the font size of the label in cell A1 to 14 points.

    e. Save your changes.

3. **Change font styles and alignment.**

    a. Apply the bold and italic font styles to the worksheet title in cell A1.

    b. Use the Merge & Center button to center the Health Insurance Premiums label over columns A–C.

    c. Apply the italic font style to the Health Insurance Premiums label.

    d. Add the bold font style to the labels in row 4.

    e. Use the Format Painter to copy the format in cell A4 to the range A5:A10.

    f. Apply the format in cell C10 to cell B14.

    g. Change the alignment of cell A10 to Align Right using a button in the Alignment group.

Skills Review (continued)

 h. Select the range of cells containing the column labels, then center them.

 i. Remove the italic font style from the Health Insurance Premiums label, then increase the font size to 14.

 j. Move the Health Insurance Premiums label to cell A3, remove the Merge & Center format, then add the bold and underline font styles.

 k. Save your changes.

4. Adjust column width.

 a. Resize column C to a width of 10.71 characters.

 b. Use the AutoFit feature to resize columns A and B.

 c. Clear the contents of cell A13 (do not delete the cell).

 d. Change the text in cell A14 to **Monthly Premium**, then change the width of the column to 25 characters.

 e. Save your changes.

5. Insert and delete rows and columns.

 a. Insert a new row between rows 5 and 6.

 b. Add a new department, **Donations**, in the newly inserted row. Enter **6** as the number of employees in the department.

 c. Copy the formula in cell C7 to C6.

 d. Add the following comment to cell A6: **New department**. Display the comment, then drag to move it out of the way, if necessary.

 e. Add a new column between the Department and Employees columns with the title **Family Coverage**, then resize the column using AutoFit.

 f. Delete the Legal row from the worksheet.

 g. Move the value in cell C14 to cell B14.

 h. Save your changes.

6. Apply colors, patterns, and borders.

 a. Add Outside Borders around the range A4:D10.

 b. Add a Bottom Double Border to cells C9 and D9 (above the calculated employee and premium totals).

 c. Apply the Aqua, Accent 5, Lighter 80% fill color to the labels in the Department column (do not include the Total label).

 d. Apply the Orange, Accent 6, Lighter 60% fill color to the range A4:D4.

 e. Change the color of the font in the range A4:D4 to Red, Accent 2, Darker 25%.

 f. Add a 12.5% Gray pattern style to cell A1.

 g. Format the range A14:B14 with a fill color of Dark Blue, Text 2, Lighter 40%, change the font color to White, Background 1, then apply the bold font style.

 h. Save your changes.

7. Apply conditional formatting.

 a. Select the range D5:D9, then create a conditional format that changes cell contents to green fill with dark green text if the value is between 150 and 275.

 b. Select the range C5:C9, then create a conditional format that changes cell contents to red text if the number of employees exceeds 10.

 c. Apply a purple gradient-filled data bar to the range C5:C9. (*Hint*: Click Purple Data Bar in the Gradient Fill section.)

 d. Use the Rules Manager to modify the conditional format in cells C5:C9 to display values greater than 10 in bold dark red text.

 e. Save your changes.

8. Rename and move a worksheet.

 a. Name the Sheet1 tab **Insurance Data**.

 b. Add a sheet to the workbook, then name the new sheet **Employee Data**.

 c. Change the Insurance Data tab color to Red, Accent 2, Lighter 40%.

Skills Review (continued)

d. Change the Employee Data tab color to Aqua, Accent 5, Lighter 40%.

e. Move the Employee Data sheet so it comes before (to the left of) the Insurance Data sheet.

f. Make the Insurance Data sheet active, enter your name in cell A20, then save your work.

9. Check spelling.

a. Move the cell pointer to cell A1.

b. Use the Find & Select feature to replace the Accounting label with **Accounting/Legal**.

c. Check the spelling in the worksheet using the spell checker, and correct any spelling errors if necessary.

d. Save your changes, then compare your Insurance Data sheet to FIGURE 3-28.

e. Preview the Insurance Data sheet in Backstage view, submit your work to your instructor as directed, then close the workbook and exit Excel.

FIGURE 3-28

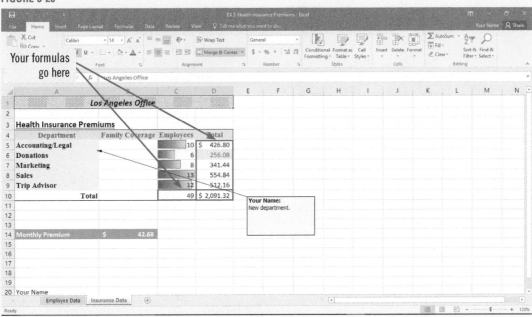

Independent Challenge 1

You run a freelance accounting business, and one of your newest clients is Fresh To You, a small local grocery store. Now that you've converted the store's accounting records to Excel, the manager would like you to work on an analysis of the inventory. Although more items will be added later, the worksheet has enough items for you to begin your modifications.

a. Start Excel, open the file EX 3-3.xlsx from the location where you store your Data Files, then save it as **EX 3-Fresh To You Inventory**.

b. Create a formula in cell E4 that calculates the value of the items in stock based on the price paid per item in cell B4. Format the cell in the Comma Style.

c. In cell F4, calculate the sale value of the items in stock using an absolute reference to the markup value shown in cell H1.

d. Copy the formulas created above into the range E5:F14; first convert any necessary cell references to absolute so that the formulas work correctly.

e. Apply bold to the column labels, and italicize the inventory items in column A.

f. Make sure that all columns are wide enough to display the data and labels.

g. Format the values in the Sale Value column as Accounting number format with two decimal places.

h. Format the values in the Price Paid column as Comma Style with two decimal places.

Independent Challenge 1 (continued)

i. Add a row under Cheddar Cheese for **Whole Wheat flour**, price paid **0.95**, sold by weight (**pound**), with **23** on hand. Copy the appropriate formulas to cells E7:F7.

j. Verify that all the data in the worksheet is visible and formulas are correct. Adjust any items as needed, and check the spelling of the entire worksheet.

k. Use conditional formatting to apply yellow fill with dark yellow text to items with a quantity of less than 25 on hand.

l. Use an icon set of your choosing in the range D4:D14 to illustrate the relative differences between values in the range.

m. Add an outside border around the data in the Item column (*do not* include the Item column label).

n. Delete the row containing the Resource Coffee - decaf entry.

o. Enter your name in an empty cell below the data, then save the file. Compare your worksheet to the sample in FIGURE 3-29.

p. Preview the worksheet in Backstage view, submit your work to your instructor as directed, close the workbook, then exit Excel.

FIGURE 3-29

Independent Challenge 2

You volunteer several hours each week with the Assistance League of San Antonio, and you are in charge of maintaining the membership list. You're currently planning a mailing campaign to members in certain regions of the city. You also want to create renewal letters for members whose membership expires soon. You decide to format the list to enhance the appearance of the worksheet and make your upcoming tasks easier to plan.

a. Start Excel, open the file EX 3-4.xlsx from the location where you store your Data Files, then save it as **EX 3-Memphis Assistance League**.

b. Remove any blank columns.

c. Create a conditional format in the Zip Code column so that entries greater than 38249 appear in light red fill with dark red text.

d. Make all columns wide enough to fit their data and labels. (*Hint*: You can use any method to size the columns.)

e. Use formatting enhancements, such as fonts, font sizes, font styles, and fill colors, to make the worksheet more attractive.

Independent Challenge 2 (continued)

f. Center the column labels.

g. Use conditional formatting so that entries for Year of Membership Expiration that are between 2021 and 2023 appear in green fill with bold black text. (*Hint*: Create a custom format for cells that meet the condition.)

h. Adjust any items as necessary, then check the spelling.

i. Change the name of the Sheet1 tab to one that reflects the sheet's contents, then add a tab color of your choice.

j. Enter your name in an empty cell, then save your work.

k. Preview the worksheet, make any final changes you think necessary, then submit your work to your instructor as directed. Compare your work to the sample shown in FIGURE 3-30.

l. Close the workbook, then exit Excel.

FIGURE 3-30

Independent Challenge 3

Advantage Calendars is a Dallas-based printer that prints and assembles calendars. As the finance manager for the company, one of your responsibilities is to analyze the monthly reports from the five district sales offices. Your boss, Joanne Bennington, has just asked you to prepare a quarterly sales report for an upcoming meeting. Because several top executives will be attending this meeting, Joanne reminds you that the report must look professional. In particular, she asks you to highlight the fact that the Northeastern district continues to outpace the other districts.

a. Plan a worksheet that shows the company's sales during the first quarter. Assume that all calendars are the same price. Make sure you include the following:

- The number of calendars sold (units sold) and the associated revenues (total sales) for each of the five district sales offices. The five sales districts are Northeastern, Midwestern, Southeastern, Southern, and Western.
- Calculations that show month-by-month totals for January, February, and March, and a 3-month cumulative total.
- Calculations that show each district's share of sales (percent of Total Sales).
- Labels that reflect the month-by-month data as well as the cumulative data.
- Formatting enhancements such as data bars that emphasize the recent month's sales surge and the Northeastern district's sales leadership.

b. Ask yourself the following questions about the organization and formatting of the worksheet: What worksheet title and labels do you need, and where should they appear? How can you calculate the totals? What formulas can you copy to save time and keystrokes? Do any of these formulas need to use an absolute reference? How do you show dollar amounts? What information should be shown in bold? Do you need to use more than one font? Should you use more than one point size?

c. Start Excel, then save a new, blank workbook as **EX 3-Advantage Calendars** to the location where you store your Data Files.

Independent Challenge 3 (continued)

d. Build the worksheet with your own price and sales data. Enter the titles and labels first, then enter the numbers and formulas. You can use the information in TABLE 3-4 to get started.

TABLE 3-4

Advantage Calendars										
1st Quarter Sales Report										
		January		February		March		Total		
Office	Price	Units Sold	Sales	Units Sold	Sales	Units Sold	Sales	Units Sold	Sales	Total % of Sales
Northeastern										
Midwestern										
Southeastern										
Southern										
Western										

e. Add a row beneath the data containing the totals for each column.

f. Adjust the column widths as necessary.

g. Change the height of row 1 to 33 points.

h. Format labels and values to enhance the look of the worksheet, and change the font styles and alignment if necessary.

i. Resize columns and adjust the formatting as necessary.

j. Add data bars for the monthly Units Sold columns.

k. Add a column that calculates a 25% increase in total sales dollars. Use an absolute cell reference in this calculation. (*Hint*: Make sure that the current formatting is applied to the new information.)

l. Delete the contents of cells J4:K4 if necessary, then merge and center cell I4 over column I:K.

m. Add a bottom double border to cells I10:L10.

n. Enter your name in an empty cell.

o. Check the spelling in the workbook, change to a landscape orientation, save your work, then compare your work to FIGURE 3-31.

p. Preview the worksheet in Backstage view, then submit your work to your instructor as directed.

q. Close the workbook file, then exit Excel.

FIGURE 3-31

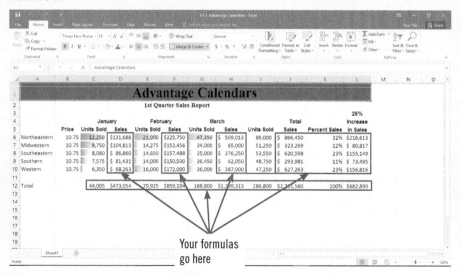

Independent Challenge 4: Explore

This Independent Challenge requires an Internet connection.

Your corporate relocation company helps employees to settle quickly and easily into new cities around the world. Your latest client plans to send employees to seven different countries. All employees will receive the same weekly budget in American currency. You need to create a worksheet to help all the employees understand the currency conversion rates in the different countries so that they can plan their spending effectively.

a. Start Excel, then save a new, blank workbook as **EX 3-Foreign Currency Rates** to the location where you store your Data Files.

b. Add a title at the top of the worksheet.

c. Think of seven countries that each use a different currency, then enter column and row labels for your worksheet. (*Hint*: You may wish to include row labels for each country, plus column labels for the country, the $1 equivalent in native currency, the total amount of native currency employees will have in each country, and the name of each country's monetary unit.)

d. Decide how much money employees will bring to each country (for example, $1,000), and enter that in the worksheet.

e. Use your favorite search engine to find your own information sources on currency conversions for the countries you have listed.

f. Enter the cash equivalent to $1 in U.S. dollars for each country in your list.

g. Create an equation that calculates the amount of native currency employees will have in each country, using an absolute cell reference in the formula.

h. Format the entries in the column containing the native currency $1 equivalent as Number number format with three decimal places, and format the column containing the total native currency budget with two decimal places, using the correct currency number format for each country. (*Hint*: Use the Number tab in the Format cells dialog box; choose the appropriate currency number format from the Symbol list.)

i. Create a conditional format that changes the font style and color of the calculated amount in the $1,000 US column to light red fill with dark red text if the amount exceeds **1000** units of the local currency.

j. Merge and center the worksheet title over the column headings.

k. Add any formatting you want to the column headings, and resize the columns as necessary.

l. Add a background color to the title and change the font color if you choose.

m. Enter your name in the header of the worksheet.

n. Spell check the worksheet, save your changes, compare your work to FIGURE 3-32, then preview the worksheet, and submit your work to your instructor as directed.

o. Close the workbook and exit Excel.

FIGURE 3-32

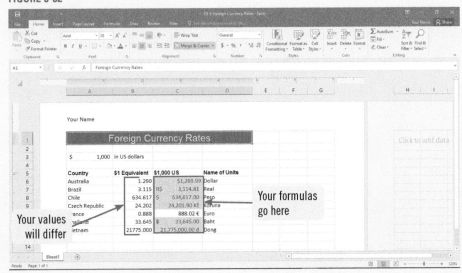

Visual Workshop

Open the file EX 3-5.xlsx from the location where you store your Data Files, then save it as **EX 3-London Employees**. Use the skills you learned in this module to format the worksheet so it looks like the one shown in **FIGURE 3-33**. Create a conditional format in the Level column so that entries greater than 3 appear in light red fill with dark red text. Create an additional conditional format in the Review Cycle column so that any value equal to 3 appears in black fill with white bold text. Replace the Accounting department label with **Legal**. (*Hint*: The only additional font used in this exercise is 18-point Times New Roman in row 1.) Enter your name in the upper-right part of the header, check the spelling in the worksheet, save your changes, then submit your work to your instructor as directed. (*Hint*: To match the figure exactly, remember to match the zoom level.)

FIGURE 3-33

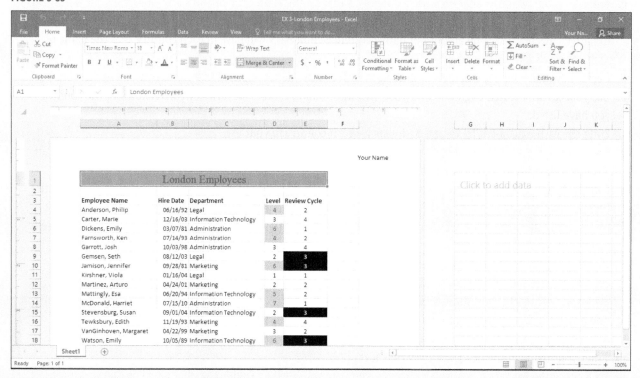

Working with Charts

CASE > At the upcoming annual meeting, Yolanda Lee wants to discuss spending patterns at Reason2Go. She asks you to create a chart showing the trends in company expenses over the past four quarters.

Module Objectives

After completing this module, you will be able to:

- Plan a chart
- Create a chart
- Move and resize a chart
- Change the chart design
- Change the chart format
- Format a chart
- Annotate and draw on a chart
- Create a pie chart

Files You Will Need

EX 4-1.xlsx	EX 4-4.xlsx
EX 4-2.xlsx	EX 4-5.xlsx
EX 4-3.xlsx	EX 4-6.xlsx

Plan a Chart

Learning
Outcomes
• Prepare to create
a chart
• Identify chart
elements
• Explore common
chart types

Before creating a chart, you need to plan the information you want your chart to show and how you want it to look. Planning ahead helps you decide what type of chart to create and how to organize the data. Understanding the parts of a chart makes it easier to format and change specific elements so that the chart best illustrates your data. **CASE** *In preparation for creating the chart for Yolanda's presentation, you identify your goals for the chart and plan its layout.*

DETAILS

Use the following guidelines to plan the chart:

• **Determine the purpose of the chart, and identify the data relationships you want to communicate graphically**

You want to create a chart that shows quarterly tour expenses for each country where Reason2Go provides tours. This worksheet data is shown in **FIGURE 4-1**. You also want the chart to illustrate whether the quarterly expenses for each country increased or decreased from quarter to quarter.

QUICK TIP
The Quick Analysis tool recommends charts based on the selected data.

• **Determine the results you want to see, and decide which chart type is most appropriate**

Different chart types display data in distinctive ways. For example, a pie chart compares parts to the whole, so it's useful for showing what proportion of a budget amount was spent on tours in one country relative to what was spent on tours in other countries. A line chart, in contrast, is best for showing trends over time. To choose the best chart type for your data, you should first decide how you want your data displayed and interpreted. **TABLE 4-1** describes several different types of charts you can create in Excel and their corresponding buttons on the Insert tab on the Ribbon. Because you want to compare R2G tour expenses in multiple countries over a period of four quarters, you decide to use a column chart.

• **Identify the worksheet data you want the chart to illustrate**

Sometimes you use all the data in a worksheet to create a chart, while at other times you may need to select a range within the sheet. The worksheet from which you are creating your chart contains expense data for each of the past four quarters and the totals for the past year. You will need to use all the quarterly data except the quarterly totals.

• **Understand the elements of a chart**

The chart shown in **FIGURE 4-2** contains basic elements of a chart. In the figure, R2G tour countries are on the horizontal axis (also called the **x-axis**) and expense dollar amounts are on the vertical axis (also called the **y-axis**). The horizontal axis is also called the **category axis** because it often contains the names of data groups, such as locations, months, or years. The vertical axis is also called the **value axis** because it often contains numerical values that help you interpret the size of chart elements. (3-D charts also contain a **z-axis**, for comparing data across both categories and values.) The area inside the horizontal and vertical axes is the **plot area**. The **tick marks**, on the vertical axis, and **gridlines** (extending across the plot area) create a scale of measure for each value. Each value in a cell you select for your chart is a **data point**. In any chart, a **data marker** visually represents each data point, which in this case is a column. A collection of related data points is a **data series**. In this chart, there are four data series (Quarter 1, Quarter 2, Quarter 3, and Quarter 4). Each is made up of column data markers of a different color, so a **legend** is included to make it easy to identify them.

FIGURE 4-1: Worksheet containing expense data

FIGURE 4-2: Chart elements

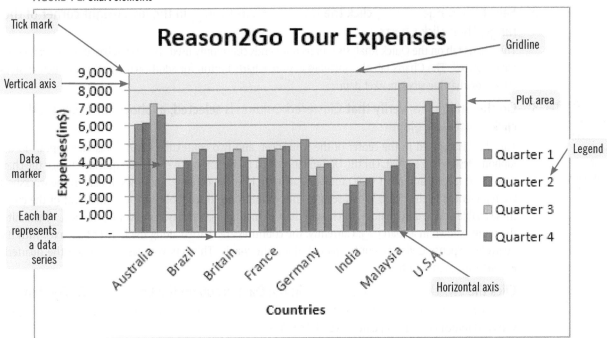

TABLE 4-1: Common chart types

type	button	description
Column		Compares data using columns; the Excel default; sometimes referred to as a bar chart in other spreadsheet programs
Line		Compares trends over even time intervals; looks similar to an area chart, but does not emphasize total
Pie		Compares sizes of pieces as part of a whole; used for a single series of numbers
Bar		Compares data using horizontal bars; sometimes referred to as a horizontal bar chart in other spreadsheet programs
Area		Shows how individual volume changes over time in relation to total volume
Scatter		Compares trends over uneven time or measurement intervals; used in scientific and engineering disciplines for trend spotting and extrapolation
Combo		Displays two or more types of data using different chart types; illustrates mixed or widely varying types of data

Create a Chart

Learning
Outcomes
• Create a chart
• Switch a chart's
  columns/rows
• Add a chart title

To create a chart in Excel, you first select the range in a worksheet containing the data you want to chart. Once you've selected a range, you can use The Quick Analysis tool or the Insert tab on the Ribbon to create a chart based on the data in the range. **CASE** *Using the worksheet containing the quarterly expense data, you create a chart that shows how the expenses in each country varied across the quarters.*

STEPS

1. **Start Excel, open the file** EX 4-1.xlsx **from the location where you store your Data Files, then save it as** EX 4-R2G Quarterly Tour Expenses
   You want the chart to include the quarterly tour expenses values, as well as quarter and country labels. You don't include the Total column and row because the figures in these cells would skew the chart.

2. **Select the range** A4:E12, **click the** Quick Analysis tool ▤ **in the lower-right corner of the range, then click** Charts
   The Charts tab on the Quick Analysis tool recommends commonly used chart types based on the range you have selected. The Charts tab also includes a More Charts button for additional chart types, such as stock charts for charting stock market data.

3. **On the** Charts tab, **verify that** Clustered Column **is selected, as shown in** FIGURE 4-3, **then click** Clustered Column
   The chart is inserted in the center of the worksheet, and two contextual Chart Tools tabs appear on the Ribbon: Design and Format. On the Design tab, which is currently active, you can quickly change the chart type, chart layout, and chart style, and you can swap how the columns and rows of data in the worksheet are represented in the chart. When seen in the Normal view, three tools display to the right of the chart: these enable you to add, remove, or change chart elements ✚ , set a style and color scheme ✎ , and filter the results shown in a chart ▼ . Currently, the countries are charted along the horizontal x-axis, with the quarterly expense dollar amounts charted along the y-axis. This lets you easily compare the quarterly expenses for each country.

4. **Click the** Switch Row/Column button **in the Data group on the Chart Tools Design tab**
   The quarters are now charted along the x-axis. The expense amounts per country are charted along the y-axis, as indicated by the updated legend. See FIGURE 4-4.

5. **Click the** Undo button ↺▾ **on the Quick Access Toolbar**
   The chart returns to its original design.

6. **Click the** Chart Title placeholder **to show the text box, click anywhere in the** Chart Title text box, **press [Ctrl][A] to select the text, type** R2G Quarterly Tour Expenses, **then click anywhere in the chart to deselect the title**
   Adding a title helps identify the chart. The border around the chart and the **sizing handles**, the small series of dots at the corners and sides of the chart's border, indicate that the chart is selected. See FIGURE 4-5. Your chart might be in a different location on the worksheet and may look slightly different; you will move and resize it in the next lesson. Any time a chart is selected, as it is now, a blue border surrounds the worksheet data range on which the chart is based, a purple border surrounds the cells containing the category axis labels, and a red border surrounds the cells containing the data series labels. This chart is known as an **embedded chart** because it is inserted directly in the current worksheet and doesn't exist in a separate file. Embedding a chart in the current sheet is the default selection when creating a chart, but you can also embed a chart on a different sheet in the workbook, or on a newly created chart sheet. A **chart sheet** is a sheet in a workbook that contains only a chart that is linked to the workbook data.

7. **Save your work**

FIGURE 4-3: Charts tab in Quick Analysis tool

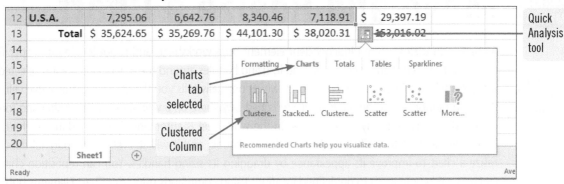

FIGURE 4-4: Clustered Column chart with different configuration of rows and columns

FIGURE 4-5: Chart with original configuration restored and title added

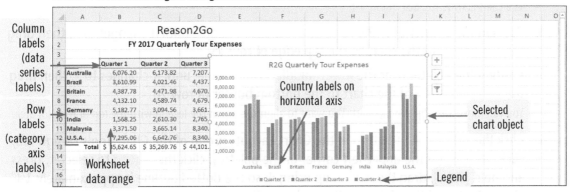

Creating sparklines

You can quickly create a miniature chart called a **sparkline** that serves as a visual indicator of data trends. You can create a sparkline by selecting a range of data, clicking the Quick Analysis tool, clicking the Sparklines tab, then clicking the type of sparkline you want. (The sparkline appears in the cell immediately adjacent to the selected range.) You can also select a range, click the Insert tab, then click the Line, Column, or Win/Loss button in the Sparklines group. In the Create Sparklines dialog box that opens, enter the cell in which you want the sparkline to appear,

then click OK. FIGURE 4-6 shows a sparkline created in a cell. Any changes to data in the range are reflected in the sparkline. To delete a selected sparkline from a cell, click the Clear button in the Group group on the Sparkline Tools Design tab.

FIGURE 4-6: Sparklines in a cell

Excel 2016

Move and Resize a Chart

Learning
Outcomes
- Reposition a chart
- Resize a chart
- Modify a legend
- Modify chart data

A chart is an **object**, or an independent element on a worksheet, and is not located in a specific cell or range. You can select an object by clicking it; sizing handles around the object indicate it is selected. (When a chart is selected in Excel, the Name box, which normally tells you the address of the active cell, tells you the chart number.) You can move a selected chart anywhere on a worksheet without affecting formulas or data in the worksheet. Any data changed in the worksheet is automatically updated in the chart. You can even move a chart to a different sheet in the workbook, and it will still reflect the original data. You can resize a chart to improve its appearance by dragging its sizing handles. You can reposition chart objects (such as a title or legend) to predefined locations using commands using the Chart Elements button or the Add Chart Element button on the Chart Tools Design tab, or you can freely move any chart object by dragging it or by cutting and pasting it to a new location. When you point to a chart object, the name of the object appears as a ScreenTip. **CASE** *You want to resize the chart, position it below the worksheet data, and move the legend.*

STEPS

QUICK TIP

To delete a selected chart, press [Delete].

1. **Make sure the chart is still selected, then position the pointer over the chart**

   The pointer shape ⊹ indicates that you can move the chart. For a table of commonly used object pointers, refer to **TABLE 4-2**.

TROUBLE

Dragging a chart element instead of a blank area moves the element instead of the chart; if this happens, undo the action and try again.

2. **Position ⊹ on a blank area near the upper-left edge of the chart, press and hold the left mouse button, drag the chart until its upper-left corner is at the upper-left corner of cell A16, then release the mouse button**

   When you release the mouse button, the chart appears in the new location.

3. **Scroll down so you can see the whole chart, position the pointer on the right-middle sizing handle until it changes to ↔, then drag the right border of the chart to the right edge of column G**

   The chart is widened. See **FIGURE 4-7**.

QUICK TIP

To resize a selected chart to an exact size, click the Chart Tools Format tab, then enter the desired height and width in the Size group.

4. **Position the pointer over the upper-middle sizing handle until it changes to ↕, then drag the top border of the chart to the top edge of row 15**

5. **Position the pointer over the lower-middle sizing handle until it changes to ↕, then drag the bottom border of the chart to the bottom border of row 26**

   You can move any object on a chart. You want to align the top of the legend with the top of the plot area.

QUICK TIP

You can move a legend to the right, top, left, or bottom of a chart by clicking Legend in the Add Chart Element button in the Chart Layouts group on the Chart Tools Design tab, then clicking a location option.

6. **Click the Quick Layout button in the Chart Layouts group of the Chart Tools Design tab, click Layout 1 (in the upper-left corner of the palette), click the legend to select it, press and hold [Shift], drag the legend up using ⊹ so the dotted outline is approximately 1/4" above the top of the plot area, then release [Shift]**

   When you click the legend, sizing handles appear around it and "Legend" appears as a ScreenTip when the pointer hovers over the object. As you drag, a dotted outline of the legend border appears. Pressing and holding the [Shift] key holds the horizontal position of the legend as you move it vertically. Although the sizing handles on objects within a chart look different from the sizing handles that surround a chart, they function the same way.

7. **Click cell A12, type United States, click the Enter button ☑ on the formula bar, use AutoFit to resize column A, then save your work**

   The axis label changes to reflect the updated cell contents, as shown in **FIGURE 4-8**. Changing any data in the worksheet modifies corresponding text or values in the chart. Because the chart is no longer selected, the Chart Tools tabs no longer appear on the Ribbon.

FIGURE 4-7: Moved and resized chart

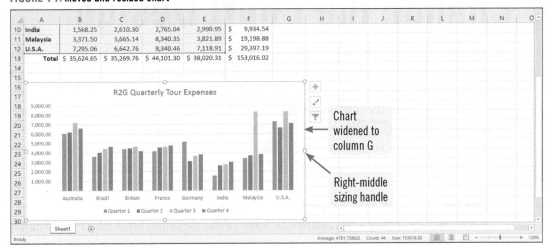

FIGURE 4-8: Worksheet with modified legend and label

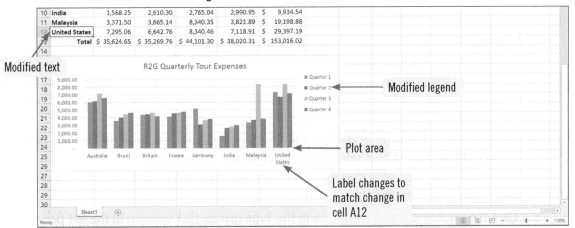

TABLE 4-2: Common object pointers

name	pointer	use	name	pointer	use
Diagonal resizing	⬉ or ⬈	Change chart shape from corners	I-beam	I	Edit object text
Draw	+	Draw an object	Move	✛	Move object
Horizontal resizing	⇔	Change object width	Vertical resizing	↕	Change object height

Moving an embedded chart to a sheet

Suppose you have created an embedded chart that you decide would look better on a chart sheet or in a different worksheet. You can make this change without recreating the entire chart. To do so, first select the chart, click the Chart Tools Design tab, then click the Move Chart button in the Location group. The Move Chart dialog box opens. To move the chart to its own chart sheet, click the New sheet option button, type a name for the new sheet if desired, then click OK. If the chart is already on its own sheet or you want to move it to a different existing sheet, click the Object in option button, click the desired worksheet, then click OK.

Change the Chart Design

Learning
Outcomes
• Change the chart
  design
• Change the chart
  type
• Apply a chart style

Once you've created a chart, you can change the chart type, modify the data range and column/row configuration, apply a different chart style, and change the layout of objects in the chart. The layouts in the Chart Layouts group on the Chart Tools Design tab offer arrangements of objects in your chart, such as its legend, title, or gridlines; choosing one of these layouts is an alternative to manually changing how objects are arranged in a chart. **CASE** *You discovered that the data for Malaysia and the United States in Quarter 3 is incorrect. After the correction, you want to see how the data looks using different chart layouts and types.*

STEPS

1. **Click cell D11, type 5568.92, press [Enter], type 7107.09, then press [Enter]**
   In the chart, the Quarter 3 data markers for Malaysia and the United States reflect the adjusted expense figures. See **FIGURE 4-9**.

2. **Select the chart by clicking a blank area within the chart border, click the Chart Tools Design tab on the Ribbon, click the Quick Layout button in the Chart Layouts group, then click Layout 3**
   The legend moves to the bottom of the chart. You prefer the original layout.

3. **Click the Undo button [↶ ▾] on the Quick Access Toolbar, then click the Change Chart Type button in the Type group**
   The Change Chart Type dialog box opens, as shown in **FIGURE 4-10**. The left pane of the dialog box lists the available categories, and the right pane shows the individual chart types. A pale gray border surrounds the currently selected chart type.

4. **Click Bar in the left pane of the Change Chart Type dialog box, confirm that the first Clustered Bar chart type is selected in the right pane, then click OK**
   The column chart changes to a clustered bar chart. See **FIGURE 4-11**. You decide to see how the data looks in a three-dimensional column chart.

5. **Click the Change Chart Type button in the Type group, click Column in the left pane of the Change Chart Type dialog box, click 3-D Clustered Column (fourth from the left in the top row) in the right pane, verify that the left-most 3-D chart is selected, then click OK**
   A three-dimensional column chart appears. You notice that the three-dimensional column format gives you a sense of volume, but it is more crowded than the two-dimensional column format.

6. **Click the Change Chart Type button in the Type group, click Clustered Column (first from the left in the top row) in the right pane of the Change Chart Type dialog box, then click OK**

7. **Click the Style 3 chart style in the Chart Styles group**
   The columns change to lighter shades of color. You prefer the previous chart style's color scheme.

8. **Click [↶ ▾] on the Quick Access Toolbar, then save your work**

Creating a combo chart

A **combo chart** presents two or more charts in one; a column chart with a line chart, for example. This type of chart is helpful when charting dissimilar but related data. For example, you can create a combo chart based on home price and home size data, showing home prices in a column chart and related home sizes in a line chart. Here a **secondary axis** (such as a vertical axis on the right side of the chart) would supply the scale for the home sizes.

To create a combo chart, select all the data you want to plot, click the Combo chart button [⯆ ▾] in the Charts group in the Insert tab, click a suggested type or Create Custom Combo Chart, supply additional series information if necessary, then click OK. To change an existing chart to a combo chart, select the chart, click Change Chart Type in the Type group on the Chart Tools Design tab, then follow the same procedure.

FIGURE 4-9: Worksheet with modified data

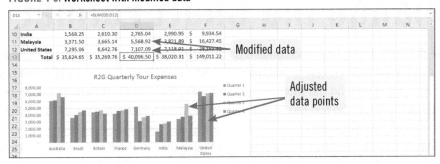

Modified data

Adjusted data points

FIGURE 4-10: Change Chart Type dialog box

Chart Type categories

Currently selected chart type

Bar chart type category

FIGURE 4-11: Column chart changed to bar chart

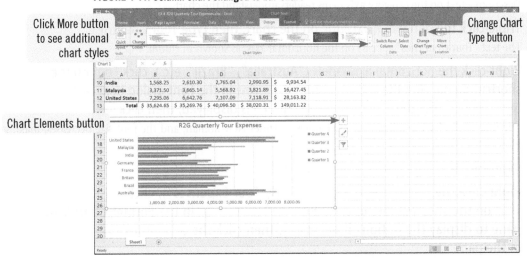

Click More button to see additional chart styles

Change Chart Type button

Chart Elements button

Working with a 3-D chart

Excel includes two kinds of 3-D chart types. In a true 3-D chart, a third axis, called the **z-axis**, lets you compare data points across both categories and values. The z-axis runs along the depth of the chart, so it appears to advance from the back of the chart. To create a true 3-D chart, look for chart types that begin with "3-D," such as 3-D Column. In a 3-D chart, data series can sometimes obscure other columns or bars in the same chart, but

you can rotate the chart to obtain a better view. Right-click the chart, then click 3-D Rotation. The Format Chart Area pane opens with the 3-D Rotation category active. The 3-D Rotation options let you change the orientation and perspective of the chart area, plot area, walls, and floor. The 3-D Format category lets you apply three-dimensional effects to selected chart objects. (Not all 3-D Rotation and 3-D Format options are available on all charts.)

Change the Chart Format

Learning
Outcomes
• Change the
  gridlines display
• Add axis titles
• Change the
  border color
• Add a shadow
  to an object

While the Chart Tools Design tab contains preconfigured chart layouts you can apply to a chart, the Chart Elements button makes it easy to add, remove, and modify individual chart objects such as a chart title or legend. Using options on this shortcut menu (or using the Add Chart Element button on the Chart Tools Design tab), you can also add text to a chart, add and modify labels, change the display of axes, modify the fill behind the plot area, create titles for the horizontal and vertical axes, and eliminate or change the look of gridlines. You can format the text in a chart object using the Home tab or the Mini toolbar, just as you would the text in a worksheet. **CASE** ▶ *You want to change the layout of the chart by creating titles for the horizontal and vertical axes. To improve the chart's appearance, you'll add a drop shadow to the chart title.*

STEPS

1. **With the chart still selected, click the** Add Chart Element button **in the Chart Layouts group on the Chart Tools Design tab, point to** Gridlines, **then click** Primary Major Horizontal **to deselect it**

   The gridlines that extend from the value axis tick marks across the chart's plot area are removed as shown in **FIGURE 4-12**.

2. **Click the** Chart Elements button ⊞ **in the upper-right corner** *outside* **the chart border, click the** Gridlines arrow, **click** Primary Major Horizontal, **click** Primary Minor Horizontal, **then click** ⊞ **to close the Chart Elements fly-out menu**

   Both major and minor gridlines now appear in the chart. **Major gridlines** represent the values at the value axis tick marks, and **minor gridlines** represent the values between the tick marks.

3. **Click** ⊞, **click the** Axis Titles checkbox **to select all the axis titles options, triple-click the** vertical axis title **on the chart, then type** Expenses (in $)

   Descriptive text on the category axis helps readers understand the chart.

4. **Triple-click the** horizontal axis title **on the chart, then type** Tour Countries

   The text "Tour Countries" appears on the horizontal axis, as shown in **FIGURE 4-13**.

5. **Right-click the** horizontal axis labels **("Australia", "Brazil", etc.), click** Font **on the shortcut menu, click the** Latin text font list arrow **in the Font dialog box, click** Times New Roman, **click the** Size down arrow **until 8 is displayed, then click** OK

   The font of the horizontal axis labels changes to Times New Roman, and the font size decreases, making more of the plot area visible.

6. **Right-click the** vertical axis labels, **then click** Reset to Match

7. **Right-click the** Chart Title **("R2G Quarterly Tour Expenses"), click** Format Chart Title **on the shortcut menu, click the** Border arrow ▶ **in the Format Chart Title pane to display the options if necessary, then click the** Solid line option button **in the pane**

   A solid border appears around the chart title with the default blue color.

8. **Click the** Effects button ⬭ **in the Format Chart Title pane, click** Shadow, **click the** Presets list arrow, **click** Offset Diagonal Bottom Right **in the Outer group (first row, first from the left), click the** Format Chart Title pane Close button ✕, **then save your work**

   A blue border with a drop shadow surrounds the title. Compare your work to **FIGURE 4-14**.

FIGURE 4-12: Gridlines removed from chart

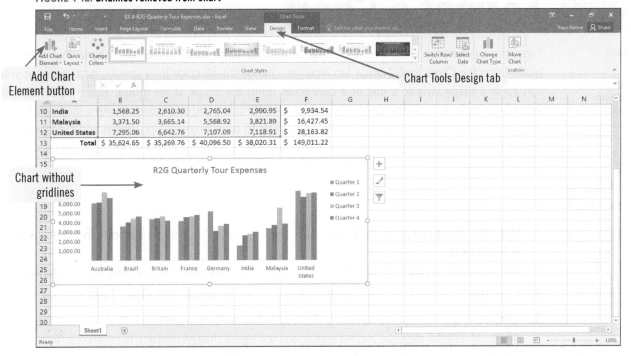

FIGURE 4-13: Axis titles added to chart

FIGURE 4-14: Enhanced chart

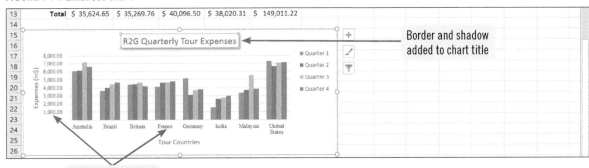

Adding data labels to a chart

There are times when your audience might benefit by seeing data labels on a chart. These labels appear next to the data markers in the chart and can indicate the series name, category name, and/or the value of one or more data points. Once your chart is selected, you can add this information to your chart by clicking the Chart Elements button in the upper-right corner outside the selected chart, clicking the Data Labels arrow, and then clicking a display option for the data labels. Once you have added the data labels, you can format them or delete individual data labels. To delete a data label, select it and then press [Delete].

Format a Chart

Learning
Outcomes
• Change the fill of
  a data series
• Use Live Preview
  to see a new data
  series color
• Apply a style to a
  data series

Formatting a chart can make it easier to read and understand. Many formatting enhancements can be made using the Chart Tools Format tab. You can change the fill color for a specific data series, or you can apply a shape style to a title or a data series using the Shape Styles group. Shape styles make it possible to apply multiple formats, such as an outline, fill color, and text color, all with a single click. You can also apply different fill colors, outlines, and effects to chart objects using arrows and buttons in the Shape Styles group. **CASE** *You want to use a different color for one data series in the chart and apply a shape style to another, to enhance the look of the chart.*

STEPS

QUICK TIP

You can change the chart type of a selected data series by clicking the Chart Tools Design tab on the Ribbon, clicking the Change Chart Type button in the Type group, selecting a chart type for that data series, then clicking OK.

1. **With the chart selected, click the** Chart Tools Format tab **on the Ribbon, then click any column in the** Quarter 4 data series

   Handles appear on each column in the Quarter 4 data series, indicating that the entire series is selected.

2. **Click the** Shape Fill list arrow **in the Shape Styles group on the Chart Tools Format tab**

3. **Click** Orange, Accent 6 **(first row, 10th from the left) as shown in** FIGURE 4-15

   All the columns for the series become orange, and the legend changes to match the new color. You can also change the color of selected objects by applying a shape style.

4. **Click any** column **in the** Quarter 3 data series

   Handles appear on each column in the Quarter 3 data series.

QUICK TIP

To apply a WordArt style to a text object (such as the chart title), select the object, then click a style in the WordArt Styles group on the Chart Tools Format tab.

5. **Click the** More button ⊽ **on the Shape Styles gallery, then** *hover the pointer* **over the** Moderate Effect – Olive Green, Accent 3 shape style **(fifth row, fourth from the left) in the gallery, as shown in** FIGURE 4-16

   Live Preview shows the data series in the chart with the shape style applied.

6. **Click the** Subtle Effect – Olive Green, Accent 3 shape style

   The style for the data series changes, as shown in **FIGURE 4-17**.

7. **Save your work**

Previewing a chart

To print or preview just a chart, select the chart (or make the chart sheet active), click the File tab, then click Print on the navigation bar. To reposition a chart by changing the page's margins, click the Show Margins button ⊞ in the lower-right corner of the Print tab to display the margins in the preview. You can drag the margin lines to the exact settings you want; as the margins change, the size and placement of the chart on the page change too.

FIGURE 4-15: New shape fill applied to data series

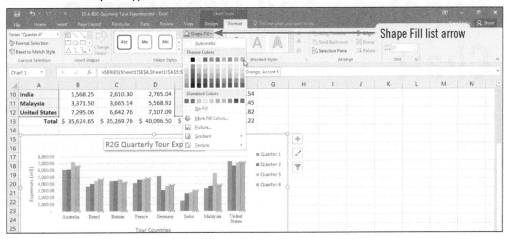

FIGURE 4-16: Live Preview of new style applied to data series

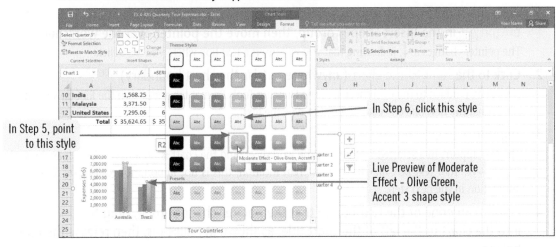

FIGURE 4-17: Style of data series changed

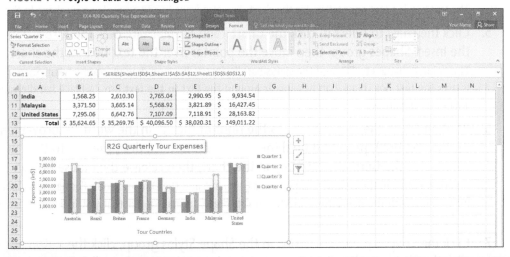

Changing alignment and angle in axis labels and titles

The buttons on the Chart Tools Design tab provide a few options for positioning axis labels and titles, but you can customize their position and rotation to exact specifications using the Format Axis pane or Format Axis Title pane. With a chart selected, right-click the axis text you want to modify, then click Format Axis or Format Axis Title on the shortcut menu. In the pane that opens, click the Size & Properties button, then select the appropriate option. You can also create a custom angle by clicking the Custom angle up and down arrows. When you have made the desired changes, close the pane.

Excel 2016

Annotate and Draw on a Chart

Learning
Outcomes
• Type text in a text box
• Draw an arrow on a chart
• Modify a drawn object

You can use text annotations and graphics to point out critical information in a chart. **Text annotations** are labels that further describe your data. You can also draw lines and arrows that point to the exact locations you want to emphasize. Shapes such as arrows and boxes can be added from the Illustrations group on the Insert tab or from the Insert Shapes group on the Chart Tools Format tab on the Ribbon. The Insert group is also used to insert pictures into worksheets and charts. **CASE** *You want to call attention to the Germany tour expense decrease, so you decide to add a text annotation and an arrow to this information in the chart.*

STEPS

1. **With the chart selected and the Chart Tools Format tab active, click the Text Box button 🔲 in the Insert Shapes group, then move the pointer over the worksheet**
   The pointer changes to ↓, indicating that you will insert a text box where you next click.

2. **Click to the right of the chart (anywhere *outside* the chart boundary)**
   A text box is added to the worksheet, and the Drawing Tools Format tab appears on the Ribbon so that you can format the new object. First you need to type the text.

3. **Type Great Improvement**
   The text appears in a selected text box on the worksheet, and the chart is no longer selected, as shown in FIGURE 4-18. Your text box may be in a different location; this is not important because you'll move the annotation in the next step.

4. **Point to an edge of the text box so that the pointer changes to 🔀, drag the text box into the chart to the left of the chart title, as shown in FIGURE 4-19, then release the mouse button**
   The text box is a text annotation for the chart. You also want to add a simple arrow shape in the chart.

5. **Click the chart to select it, click the Chart Tools Format tab, click the Arrow button ◥ in the Insert Shapes group, then move the pointer over the text box on the chart**
   The pointer changes to ✛, and the status bar displays "Click and drag to insert an AutoShape." When ✛ is over the text box, black handles appear around the text in the text box. A black handle can act as an anchor for the arrow.

6. **Position ✛ on the black handle to the right of the "t" in the word "improvement" (in the text box), press and hold the left mouse button, drag the line to the Quarter 2 column for the Germany category in the chart, then release the mouse button**
   An arrow points to the Quarter 2 expense for Germany, and the Drawing Tools Format tab displays options for working with the new arrow object. You can resize, format, or delete it just like any other object in a chart.

7. **Click the Shape Outline list arrow in the Shape Styles group, click the Automatic color, click the Shape Outline list arrow again, point to Weight, then click 1½ pt**
   Compare your finished chart to FIGURE 4-20.

8. **Save your work**

FIGURE 4-18: Text box added

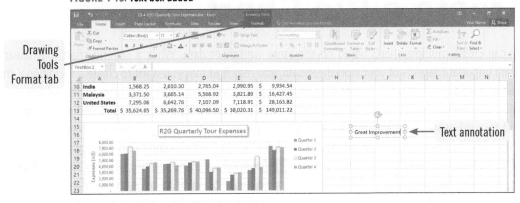

FIGURE 4-19: Text annotation on the chart

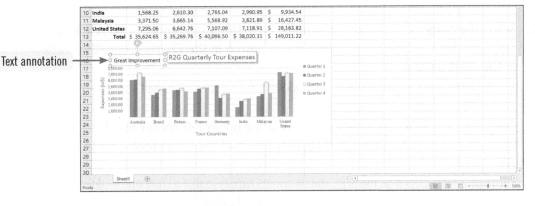

FIGURE 4-20: Arrow shape added to chart

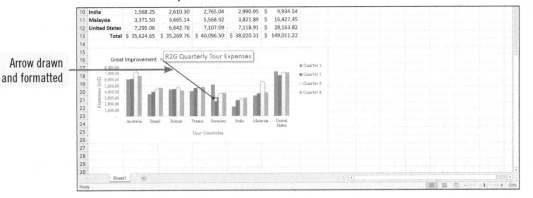

Adding SmartArt graphics

In addition to charts, annotations, and drawn objects, you can create a variety of diagrams using SmartArt graphics. **SmartArt graphics** are available in List, Process, Cycle, Hierarchy, Relationship, Matrix, Pyramid, Picture, and Office.com categories. To insert SmartArt, click the Insert a SmartArt Graphic button in the Illustrations group on the Insert tab to open the Choose a SmartArt Graphic dialog box. Click a SmartArt category in the left pane, then click a layout for the graphic in the right pane. The right pane shows sample layouts for the selected SmartArt, as shown in **FIGURE 4-21**. The SmartArt graphic appears in the worksheet as an embedded object with sizing handles. Depending on the type of SmartArt graphic you selected, a text pane opens next to the graphic; you can enter text into the graphic using the text pane or by typing directly in the shapes in the diagram.

FIGURE 4-21: Choose a SmartArt Graphic dialog box

Create a Pie Chart

Learning
Outcomes
• Create a pie chart
• Explode a pie
  chart slice

You can create multiple charts based on the same worksheet data. While a column chart may illustrate certain important aspects of your worksheet data, you may find that you want to create an additional chart to emphasize a different point. Depending on the type of chart you create, you have additional options for calling attention to trends and patterns. For example, if you create a pie chart, you can emphasize one data point by **exploding**, or pulling that slice away from, the pie chart. When you're ready to print a chart, you can preview it just as you do a worksheet to check the output before committing it to paper. You can print a chart by itself or as part of the worksheet. **CASE** ▶ *At an upcoming meeting, Yolanda plans to discuss the total tour expenses and which countries need improvement. You want to create a pie chart she can use to illustrate total expenses. Finally, you want to fit the worksheet and the charts onto one worksheet page.*

STEPS

1. **Select the range** A5:A12, **press and hold** [Ctrl], **select the range** F5:F12, **click the** Insert tab, **click the** Insert Pie or Doughnut Chart button **in the Charts group, then click** 3-D Pie **in the chart gallery**

   The new chart appears in the center of the worksheet. You can move the chart and quickly format it using a chart layout.

2. **Drag the** chart **so its upper-left corner is at the upper-left corner of cell** G1, **click the** Quick Layout button **in the Chart Layouts group of the Chart Tools Design tab, then click** Layout 2

   The chart is repositioned on the page, and its layout changes so that a chart title is added, the percentages display on each slice, and the legend appears just below the chart title.

3. **Select the** Chart Title text, **then type** R2G Total Expenses, by Country

4. **Click the slice for the** India data point, **click it again so it is the only slice selected, right-click it, then click** Format Data Point

   The Format Data Point pane opens, as shown in **FIGURE 4-22**. You can use the Point Explosion slider to control the distance a pie slice moves away from the pie, or you can type a value in the Point Explosion text box.

5. **Double-click** 0 **in the** Point Explosion text box, **type** 40, **then click the** Close button ☒

   Compare your chart to **FIGURE 4-23**. You decide to preview the chart and data before you print.

6. **Click cell** A1, **switch to** Page Layout view, **type your name in the left header text box, then click cell** A1

   You decide the chart and data would fit better on the page if they were printed in landscape orientation.

7. **Click the** Page Layout tab, **click the** Orientation button **in the Page Setup group, then click** Landscape

8. **Click the** File tab, **click** Print **on the navigation bar, verify that the correct printer is selected, click the** No Scaling setting **in the Settings section on the Print tab, then click** Fit Sheet on One Page

   The data and chart are positioned horizontally on a single page, as shown in **FIGURE 4-24**. The printer you have selected may affect the appearance of your preview screen.

9. **Save and close the workbook, submit your work to your instructor as directed, then exit Excel**

FIGURE 4-22: Format Data Point pane

Point
Explosion
slider

Point
Explosion
text box

FIGURE 4-23: Exploded pie slice

FIGURE 4-24: Preview of worksheet with charts in Backstage view

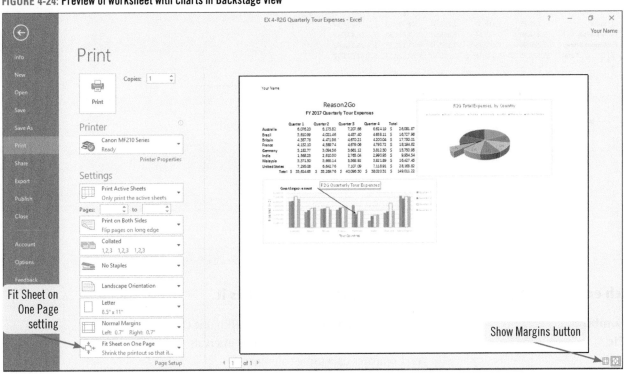

Fit Sheet on
One Page
setting

Show Margins button

Using the Insert Chart dialog box to discover new chart types

Excel 2016 includes five new chart types. You can explore these charts by clicking the Insert tab on the Ribbon, clicking Recommended Charts, then clicking the All Charts tab in the Insert Chart dialog box. Near the bottom of the list in the left panel are the new chart types: Treemap (which has nine variations), Sunburst, Histogram, Box & Whisker, and Waterfall. If cells are selected prior to opening the Insert Chart dialog box, you will see a sample of the chart type when you click each chart type; the sample will be magnified when you hover the mouse over the sample. The Treemap and Sunburst charts both offer visual comparisons of relative sizes. The Histogram looks like a column chart, but each column (or bin) represents a range of values. The Box & Whisker chart shows distribution details as well as the mean, quartiles, and outliers. The Waterfall chart shows results above and below an imaginary line.

Practice

Concepts Review

Label each element of the Excel chart shown in FIGURE 4-25.

FIGURE 4-25

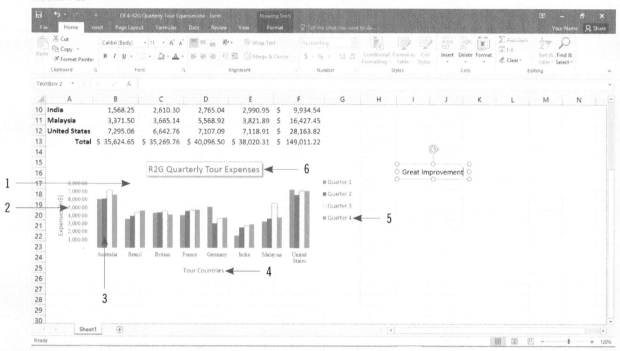

Match each chart type with the statement that best describes it.

7. Combo
8. Pie
9. Area
10. Column
11. Line

a. Displays different chart types within one chart
b. Compares trends over even time intervals
c. Compares data using columns
d. Compares data as parts of a whole
e. Shows how volume changes over time

Select the best answer from the list of choices.

12. **Which tab on the Ribbon do you use to create a chart?**
    a. Design
    b. Insert
    c. Page Layout
    d. Format

13. **A collection of related data points in a chart is called a:**
    a. Data series.
    b. Data tick.
    c. Cell address.
    d. Value title.

14. **The object in a chart that identifies the colors used for each data series is a(n):**
    a. Data marker.
    b. Data point.
    c. Organizer.
    d. Legend.

15. **How do you move an embedded chart to a chart sheet?**
    a. Click a button on the Chart Tools Design tab.
    b. Drag the chart to the sheet tab.
    c. Delete the chart, switch to a different sheet, then create a new chart.
    d. Use the Copy and Paste buttons on the Ribbon.

16. **Which is *not* an example of a SmartArt graphic?**
    a. Sparkline
    b. Basic Matrix
    c. Organization Chart
    d. Basic Pyramid

17. **Which tab appears only when a chart is selected?**
    a. Insert
    b. Chart Tools Format
    c. Review
    d. Page Layout

Skills Review

1. **Plan a chart.**
   a. Start Excel, open the Data File EX 4-2.xlsx from the location where you store your Data Files, then save it as **EX 4-Software Usage Polling Results**.
   b. Describe the type of chart you would use to plot this data.
   c. What chart type would you use to compare the number of Excel users in each type of business?

2. **Create a chart.**
   a. In the worksheet, select the range containing all the data and headings.
   b. Click the Quick Analysis tool.
   c. Create a Clustered Column chart, then add the chart title **Software Usage, by Business** above the chart.
   d. If necessary, click the Switch Row/Column button so the business type (Accounting, Advertising, etc.) appears as the x-axis.
   e. Save your work.

Skills Review (continued)

3. **Move and resize a chart.**
   a. Make sure the chart is still selected, and close any open panes if necessary.
   b. Move the chart beneath the worksheet data.
   c. Widen the chart so it extends to the right edge of column H.
   d. Use the Quick Layout button in the Chart Tools Design tab to move the legend to the right of the charted data. (*Hint*: Use Layout 1.)
   e. Resize the chart so its bottom edge is at the top of row 25.
   f. Save your work.

4. **Change the chart design.**
   a. Change the value in cell B3 to **8**. Observe the change in the chart.
   b. Select the chart.
   c. Use the Quick Layout button in the Chart Layouts group on the Chart Tools Design tab to apply the Layout 10 layout to the chart, then undo the change.
   d. Use the Change Chart Type button on the Chart Tools Design tab to change the chart to a Clustered Bar chart.
   e. Change the chart to a 3-D Clustered Column chart, then change it back to a Clustered Column chart.
   f. Save your work.

5. **Change the chart layout.**
   a. Use the Chart Elements button to turn off the primary major horizontal gridlines in the chart.
   b. Change the font used in the horizontal and vertical axis labels to Times New Roman.
   c. Turn on the primary major gridlines for both the horizontal and vertical axes.
   d. Change the chart title's font to Times New Roman if necessary, with a font size of 20.
   e. Insert **Business** as the primary horizontal axis title.
   f. Insert **Number of Users** as the primary vertical axis title.
   g. Change the font size of the horizontal and vertical axis titles to 10 and the font to Times New Roman, if necessary.
   h. Change "Personnel" in the worksheet column heading to **Human Resources**, then AutoFit column D, and any other columns as necessary.
   i. Change the font size of the legend to 14.
   j. Add a solid line border in the default color and a (preset) Offset Diagonal Bottom Right shadow to the chart title.
   k. Save your work.

6. **Format a chart.**
   a. Make sure the chart is selected, then select the Chart Tools Format tab, if necessary.
   b. Change the shape fill of the Excel data series to Dark Blue, Text 2.
   c. Change the shape style of the Excel data series to Subtle Effect – Orange, Accent 6.
   d. Save your work.

7. **Annotate and draw on a chart.**
   a. Make sure the chart is selected, then create the text annotation **Needs more users**.
   b. Position the text annotation so the word "Needs" is just below the word "Software" in the chart title.
   c. Select the chart, then use the Chart Tools Format tab to create a 1½ pt weight dark blue arrow that points from the bottom center of the text box to the Excel users in the Human Resources category.
   d. Deselect the chart.
   e. Save your work.

Skills Review (continued)

8. Create a pie chart.

- **a.** Select the range A1:F2, then create a 3-D Pie chart.
- **b.** Drag the 3-D pie chart beneath the existing chart.
- **c.** Change the chart title to **Excel Users**.
- **d.** Apply the Style 7 chart style to the chart, then apply Layout 6 using the Quick Layout button.
- **e.** Explode the Human Resources slice from the pie chart at **25%**.
- **f.** In Page Layout view, enter your name in the left section of the worksheet header.
- **g.** Preview the worksheet and charts in Backstage view, make sure all the contents fit on one page, then submit your work to your instructor as directed. When printed, the worksheet should look like FIGURE 4-26. (Note that certain elements such as the title may look slightly different when printed.)
- **h.** Save your work, close the workbook, then exit Excel.

FIGURE 4-26

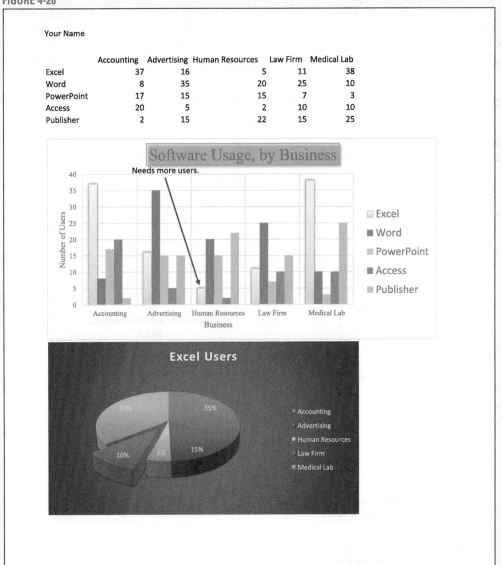

Your Name

	Accounting	Advertising	Human Resources	Law Firm	Medical Lab
Excel	37	16	5	11	38
Word	8	35	20	25	10
PowerPoint	17	15	15	7	3
Access	20	5	2	10	10
Publisher	2	15	22	15	25

Independent Challenge 1

You are the operations manager for the Chicago Arts Alliance. Each year the group revisits the number and types of activities they support to better manage their budgets. For this year's budget, you need to create charts to document the number of events in previous years.

a. Start Excel, open the file EX 4-3.xlsx from the location where you store your Data Files, then save it as **EX 4-Chicago Arts Alliance**.

b. Take some time to plan your charts. Which type of chart or charts might best illustrate the information you need to display? What kind of chart enhancements do you want to use? Will a 3-D effect make your chart easier to understand?

c. Create a Clustered Column chart for the data.

d. Change at least one of the colors used in a data series.

e. Make the appropriate modifications to the chart to make it visually attractive and easier to read and understand. Include a legend to the right of the chart, and add chart titles and horizontal and vertical axis titles using the text shown in **TABLE 4-3**.

TABLE 4-3

title	text
Chart title	Chicago Arts Alliance Events
Vertical axis title	Number of Events
Horizontal axis title	Types of Events

f. Create at least two additional charts for the same data to show how different chart types display the same data. Reposition each new chart so that all charts are visible in the worksheet. One of the additional charts should be a pie chart for an appropriate data set; the other is up to you.

g. Modify each new chart as necessary to improve its appearance and effectiveness. A sample worksheet containing three charts based on the worksheet data is shown in **FIGURE 4-27**.

h. Enter your name in the worksheet header.

i. Save your work. Before printing, preview the worksheet in Backstage view, then adjust any settings as necessary so that all the worksheet data and charts will print on a single page.

j. Submit your work to your instructor as directed.

k. Close the workbook, then exit Excel.

FIGURE 4-27

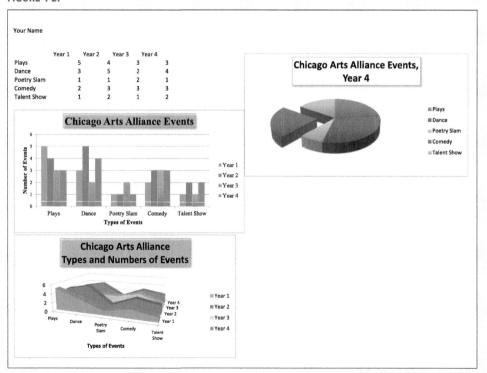

Independent Challenge 2

You work at Canine Companions, a locally owned dog obedience school. One of your responsibilities at the school is to manage the company's sales and expenses using Excel. As part of your efforts, you want to help the staff better understand and manage the school's largest sources of both expenses and sales. To do this, you've decided to create charts using current operating expenses including rent, utilities, and payroll. The manager will use these charts at the next monthly meeting.

a. Start Excel, open EX 4-4.xlsx from the location where you store your Data Files, then save it as **EX 4-Canine Companions Expense Analysis**.

b. Decide which data in the worksheet should be charted. What chart types are best suited for the information you need to show? What kinds of chart enhancements are necessary?

c. Create a 3-D Clustered Column chart in the worksheet showing the expense data for all four quarters. (*Hint*: The expense categories should appear on the x-axis. Do not include the totals.)

d. Change the vertical axis labels (Expenses data) so that no decimals are displayed. (*Hint*: Use the Number category in the Format Axis pane.)

e. Using the sales data, create two charts on this worksheet that compare the sales amounts. (*Hint*: Move each chart to a new location on the worksheet, then deselect it before creating the next one.)

f. In one chart of the sales data, add data labels, then add chart titles as you see fit.

g. Make any necessary formatting changes to make the charts look more attractive, then enter your name in a worksheet cell.

h. Save your work.

i. Preview each chart in Backstage view, and adjust any items as needed. Fit the worksheet to a single page, then submit your work to your instructor as directed. A sample of a printed worksheet is shown in **FIGURE 4-28**.

j. Close the workbook, then exit Excel.

FIGURE 4-28

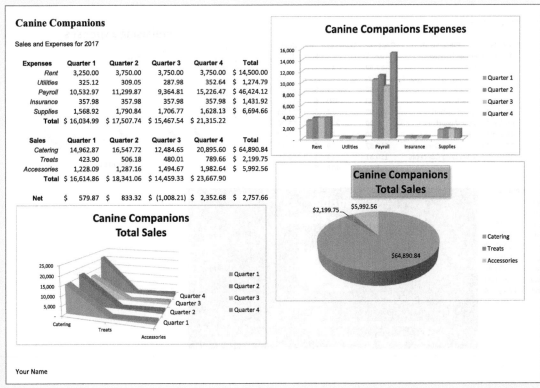

Independent Challenge 3

You are working as an account representative at a clothing store called Zanzibar. You have been examining the advertising expenses incurred recently. The CEO wants to examine expenses designed to increase sales and has asked you to prepare charts that can be used in this evaluation. In particular, you want to see how dollar amounts compare among the different expenses, and you also want to see how expenses compare with each other proportional to the total budget.

a. Start Excel, open the Data File EX 4-5.xlsx from the location where you store your Data Files, then save it as **EX 4-Zanzibar Advertising Expenses**.

b. Identify three types of charts that seem best suited to illustrate the data in the range A16:B24. What kinds of chart enhancements are necessary?

c. Create at least two different types of charts that show the distribution of advertising expenses. (*Hint*: Move each chart to a new location on the same worksheet.) One of the charts should be a 3-D pie chart.

d. In at least one of the charts, add annotated text and arrows highlighting important data, such as the largest expense.

e. Change the color of at least one data series in at least one of the charts.

f. Add chart titles and category and value axis titles where appropriate. Format the titles with a font of your choice. Apply a shadow to the chart title in at least one chart.

g. Add your name to a section of the header, then save your work.

h. Explode a slice from the 3-D pie chart.

i. Add a data label to the exploded pie slice.

j. Preview the worksheet in Backstage view. Adjust any items as needed. Be sure the charts are all visible on one page. Compare your work to the sample in **FIGURE 4-29**.

k. Submit your work to your instructor as directed, close the workbook, then exit Excel.

FIGURE 4-29

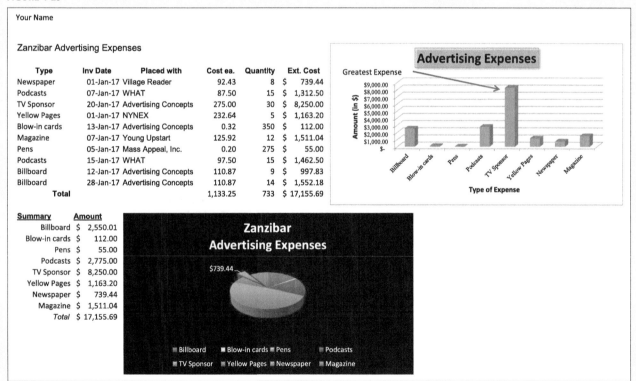

Independent Challenge 4: Explore

This Independent Challenge requires an Internet connection.

All the years of hard work and saving money have paid off, and you have decided to purchase a home. You know where you'd like to live, and you decide to use the web to find out more about houses that are currently available. A worksheet would be a great place to compare the features and prices of potential homes.

a. Start Excel, then save a new, blank workbook as **EX 4-My New House** to the location where you save your Data Files.

b. Decide on where you would like to live, and use your favorite search engine to find information sources on homes for sale in that area. (*Hint*: Try using realtor.com or other realtor-sponsored sites.)

c. Determine a price range and features within the home. Find data for at least five homes that meet your location and price requirements, and enter them in the worksheet. See **TABLE 4-4** for a suggested data layout.

TABLE 4-4

suggested data layout					
Location					
Price range					
	House 1	House 2	House 3	House 4	House 5
Asking price					
Bedrooms					
Bathrooms					
Year built					
Size (in sq. ft.)					

d. Format the data so it looks attractive and professional.

e. Create any type of column chart using only the House and Asking Price data. Place it on the same worksheet as the data. Include a descriptive title.

f. Change the colors in the chart using the chart style of your choice.

g. Enter your name in a section of the header.

h. Create an additional chart: a combo chart that plots the asking price on one axis and the size of the home on the other axis. (*Hint*: Use the Tell me what you want to do text box above the Ribbon to get more guidance on creating a Combo Chart.)

i. Save the workbook. Preview the worksheet in Backstage view and make adjustments if necessary to fit all of the information on one page. See **FIGURE 4-30** for an example of what your worksheet might look like.

j. Submit your work to your instructor as directed.

k. Close the workbook, then exit Excel.

FIGURE 4-30

Visual Workshop

Open the Data File EX 4-6.xlsx from the location where you store your Data Files, then save it as **EX 4-Estimated Cost Center Expenses**. Format the worksheet data so it looks like FIGURE 4-31, then create and modify two charts to match the ones shown in the figure. You will need to make formatting, layout, and design changes once you create the charts. (*Hint*: The shadow used in the 3-D pie chart title is made using the Outer Offset Diagonal Top Right shadow.) Enter your name in the left text box of the header, then save and preview the worksheet. Submit your work to your instructor as directed, then close the workbook and exit Excel.

FIGURE 4-31

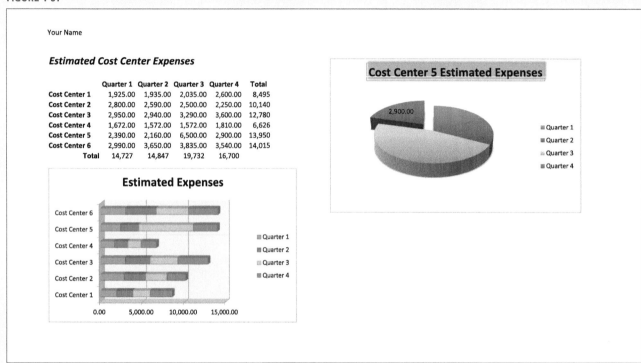

Analyzing Data Using Formulas

CASE ▶ Mary Watson, Reason2Go's vice president of sales and marketing, uses Excel formulas and functions to analyze sales data for the U.S. region and to consolidate sales data from branch offices. Because management is considering adding a new regional branch, Mary asks you to estimate the loan costs for a new office facility and to compare sales in the existing U.S. offices.

Module Objectives

After completing this module, you will be able to:

- Format data using text functions
- Sum a data range based on conditions
- Consolidate data using a formula
- Check formulas for errors
- Construct formulas using named ranges
- Build a logical formula with the IF function
- Build a logical formula with the AND function
- Calculate payments with the PMT function

Files You Will Need

EX 5-1.xlsx   EX 5-5.xlsx
EX 5-2.xlsx   EX 5-6.xlsx
EX 5-3.xlsx   EX 5-7.xlsx
EX 5-4.xlsx

Format Data Using Text Functions

Learning Outcomes

- Separate text data using Flash Fill
- Format text data using the PROPER function
- Format text data using the CONCATENATE function

Often, you need to import data into Excel from an outside source, such as another program or the Internet. Sometimes you need to reformat this data to make it understandable and attractive. Instead of handling these formatting tasks manually in each cell, you can use Excel text functions to perform them automatically for an entire range. The Flash Fill feature can be used to break data fields in one column into separate columns. The text function PROPER capitalizes the first letter in a string of text as well as any text following a space. You can use the CONCATENATE function to join two or more strings into one text string. **CASE** ▶ *Mary has received the U.S. sales representatives' data from the Human Resources Department, and has imported it into Excel. She asks you to use text formulas to format the data into a more useful layout.*

STEPS

1. Start Excel, open EX 5-1.xlsx from the location where you store your Data Files, then save it as EX 5-Sales

2. On the Sales Reps sheet, click cell B4, type troy silva, press [Tab], type new york, press [Tab], type 5, then click the Enter button ☑ on the formula bar

   You are manually separating the data in cell A4 into the adjacent cells, as shown in **FIGURE 5-1**. You will let Excel follow your pattern for the rows below using Flash Fill. **Flash Fill** uses worksheet data you have entered as an example to predict what should be entered into similar column cells.

3. With cell D4 selected, click the Data tab, then click the Flash Fill button in the Data Tools group

   The years of service number is copied from cell D4 into the range D5:D15. You will use Flash Fill to fill in the names and cities.

> **QUICK TIP**
> You can move the Function Arguments dialog box if it overlaps a cell or range that you need to click. You can also click the Collapse Dialog box button 🔳, select the cell or range, then click the Expand Dialog box button 🔳 to return to the Function Arguments dialog box.

4. Click cell B4, click the Flash Fill button in the Data Tools group, click cell C4, then click the Flash Fill button again

   The column A data is separated into columns B, C and D. You want to format the letters in the names and cities to the correct cases.

5. Click cell E4, click the Formulas tab, click the Text button in the Function Library group, click PROPER, with the insertion point in the Text text box click cell B4, then click OK

   The name is copied from cell B4 to cell E4 with the correct uppercase letters for proper names. The name is formatted in green, taking on the column's previously applied formatting.

6. Drag the fill handle to copy the formula in cell E4 to cell F4, then copy the formulas in cells E4:F4 into the range E5:F15

   You want to format the years data to be more descriptive.

> **QUICK TIP**
> Excel automatically inserts quotation marks to enclose the space and the Years text.

7. Click cell G4, click the Text button in the Function Library group, click CONCATENATE, with the insertion point in the Text1 text box click cell D4, press [Tab], with the insertion point in the Text2 text box press [Spacebar], type Years, then click OK

8. Copy the formula in cell G4 into the range G5:G15, click cell A1, compare your work to **FIGURE 5-2**, click the Insert tab, click the Header & Footer button in the Text group, click the Go to Footer button in the Navigation group, enter your name in the center text box, click on the worksheet, scroll up and click cell A1, then click the Normal button 🔲 in the Workbook Views group on the View tab

9. Save your file, then preview the worksheet

FIGURE 5-1: Worksheet with data separated into columns

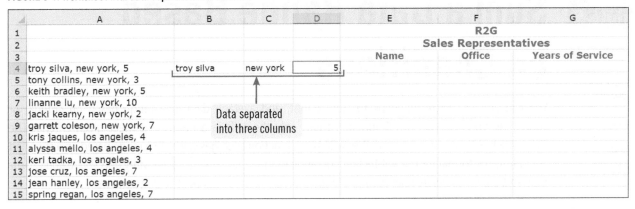

FIGURE 5-2: Worksheet with data formatted in columns

A	B	C	D	E	F	G
					R2G	
					Sales Representatives	
				Name	Office	Years of Service
troy silva, new york, 5	troy silva	new york	5	Troy Silva	New York	5 Years
tony collins, new york, 3	tony collins	new york	3	Tony Collins	New York	3 Years
keith bradley, new york, 5	keith bradley	new york	5	Keith Bradley	New York	5 Years
linanne lu, new york, 10	linanne lu	new york	10	Linanne Lu	New York	10 Years
jacki kearny, new york, 2	jacki kearny	new york	2	Jacki Kearny	New York	2 Years
garrett coleson, new york, 7	garrett coleson	new york	7	Garrett Coleson	New York	7 Years
kris jaques, los angeles, 4	kris jaques	los angeles	4	Kris Jaques	Los Angeles	4 Years
alyssa mello, los angeles, 4	alyssa mello	los angeles	4	Alyssa Mello	Los Angeles	4 Years
keri tadka, los angeles, 3	keri tadka	los angeles	3	Keri Tadka	Los Angeles	3 Years
jose cruz, los angeles, 7	jose cruz	los angeles	7	Jose Cruz	Los Angeles	7 Years
jean hanley, los angeles, 2	jean hanley	los angeles	2	Jean Hanley	Los Angeles	2 Years
spring regan, los angeles, 7	spring regan	los angeles	7	Spring Regan	Los Angeles	7 Years

Working with text in other ways

Other useful text functions include UPPER, LOWER, and SUBSTITUTE. The UPPER function converts text to all uppercase letters, the LOWER function converts text to all lowercase letters, and SUBSTITUTE replaces text in a text string. For example, if cell A1 contains the text string "Today is Wednesday", then =LOWER(A1) would produce "today is wednesday"; =UPPER(A1) would produce "TODAY IS WEDNESDAY"; and =SUBSTITUTE(A1, "Wednesday", "Tuesday") would result in "Today is Tuesday". You can also use functions to display one or more characters at certain locations within a string. Use the RIGHT function to find the last characters with the syntax =RIGHT(string, # characters), the LEFT function to find the first characters with the syntax =LEFT(string, # characters), or the MID function to display the middle characters with the syntax =MID(string, starting character, # characters). You can separate text data stored in one column into multiple columns by clicking the Data tab, clicking the Text to Columns button in the Data Tools group, and specifying the delimiter for your data. A **delimiter** is a separator, such as a space, comma, or semicolon, that should separate your data. Excel then separates your data into columns at the delimiter.

Sum a Data Range Based on Conditions

You can also use Excel functions to sum, count, and average data in a range based on criteria, or conditions, you set. The SUMIF function totals only the cells in a range that meet given criteria. The COUNTIF function counts cells and the AVERAGEIF function averages values in a range based on a specified condition. The format for the SUMIF function appears in **FIGURE 5-3**. **CASE** ▶ *Mary asks you to analyze the New York branch's January sales data to provide her with information about each experience.*

STEPS

1. **Click the NY sheet tab, click cell G7, click the Formulas tab, click the More Functions button in the Function Library group, point to Statistical, scroll down the list of functions if necessary, then click COUNTIF**

   You want to count the number of times Wildlife Care appears in the Experience Category column. The formula you use will say, in effect, "Examine the range I specify, then count the number of cells in that range that contain "Wildlife Care."" You will specify absolute addresses for the range so you can copy the formula later on in the worksheet when the same range will be used.

2. **With the insertion point in the Range text box select the range A6:A25, press [F4], press [Tab], with the insertion point in the Criteria text box, click cell F7, then click OK**

   Your formula, as shown in the formula bar in **FIGURE 5-4**, asks Excel to search the range A6:A25, and where it finds the value shown in cell F7 (that is, when it finds the value "Wildlife Care"), to add one to the total count. The number of Wildlife Care experiences, 4, appears in cell G7. You want to calculate the total sales revenue for the Wildlife Care experiences.

3. **Click cell H7, click the Math & Trig button in the Function Library group, scroll down the list of functions, then click SUMIF**

   The Function Arguments dialog box opens. You want to enter two ranges and a criterion; the first range is the one where you want Excel to search for the criteria entered. The second range contains the corresponding cells that Excel will total when it finds the criterion you specify in the first range.

4. **With the insertion point in the Range text box, select the range A6:A25, press [F4], press [Tab], with the insertion point in the Criteria text box click cell F7, press [Tab], with the insertion point in the Sum_range text box select the range B6:B25, press [F4], then click OK**

   Your formula asks Excel to search the range A6:A25, and where it finds Wildlife Care to add the corresponding amounts from column B. The revenue for the Wildlife Care experiences, $4,603, appears in cell H7. You want to calculate the average price paid for the Wildlife Care experiences.

5. **Click cell I7, click the More Functions button in the Function Library group, point to Statistical, then click AVERAGEIF**

6. **With the insertion point in the Range text box select the range A6:A25, press [F4], press [Tab], with the insertion point in the Criteria text box click cell F7, press [Tab], with the insertion point in the Average_range text box select the range B6:B25, press [F4], then click OK**

   The average price paid for the Wildlife Care experiences, $1,151, appears in cell I7.

7. **Select the range G7:I7, then drag the fill handle to fill the range G8:I10**

   Compare your results with those in **FIGURE 5-5**.

8. **Add your name to the center of the footer, save the workbook, then preview the sheet**

FIGURE 5-3: Format of SUMIF function

SUMIF(range, criteria, [sum_range])

| The range the function searches | The condition that must be satisfied in the range | The range where the cells that meet the condition will be totaled |

FIGURE 5-4: COUNTIF function in the formula bar

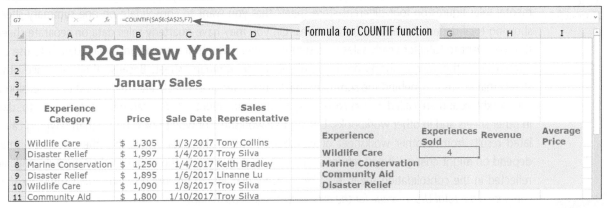

Formula for COUNTIF function

FIGURE 5-5: Worksheet with conditional statistics

Experience	Experiences Sold	Revenue	Average Price
Wildlife Care	4	$ 4,603	$1,151
Marine Conservation	5	$ 5,613	$1,123
Community Aid	5	$ 9,016	$1,803
Disaster Relief	6	$ 11,864	$1,977

Entering date and time functions

Microsoft Excel stores dates as sequential serial numbers and uses them in calculations. January 1, 1900 is assigned serial number 1 and numbers are represented as the number of days following that date. You can see the serial number of a date by using the DATE function. For example, to see the serial number of January, 1, 2017 you would enter =DATE(2017,1,1). The result would be in date format, but if you formatted the cell as Number, it would display the serial number 42736 for this date. Because Excel uses serial numbers, you can perform calculations that include dates and times using the Excel date and time functions. To enter a date or time function, click the Formulas tab on the Ribbon, click the Date & Time button in the Function Library group, then click the Date or Time function you want. All of the date and time functions will be displayed as dates and times unless you change the formatting to Number. See TABLE 5-1 for some of the available Date and Time functions in Excel.

TABLE 5-1: Date and Time functions

function	calculates	example
TODAY	The current date	=TODAY()
NOW	The current date and time	=NOW()
DATE	Displays a date you enter	=DATE(2017,1,2)
TIME	A serial number from hours, minutes, and seconds	=TIME(5,12,20)
YEAR	A year portion of a date	=YEAR(1/20/2017)
HOUR	The hour portion of a time	=HOUR("15:30:30")
MINUTE	The minute portion of a time	=MINUTE("15:30:30")

Excel 2016

Learning
Outcomes
• Consolidate data
  on multiple sheets
  using AutoSum
• Consolidate data on
  multiple sheets
  using 3-D references

Consolidate Data Using a Formula

When you want to summarize similar data that exists in different sheets or workbooks, you can **consolidate**, or combine and display, the data in one sheet. For example, you might have entered departmental sales figures on four different store sheets that you want to consolidate on one summary sheet, showing total departmental sales for all stores. Or, you may have quarterly sales data on separate sheets that you want to total for yearly sales on a summary sheet. The best way to consolidate data is to use cell references to the various sheets on a consolidation, or summary, sheet. Because they reference other sheets that are usually behind the summary sheet, such references effectively create another dimension in the workbook and are called **3-D references**, as shown in FIGURE 5-6. You can reference, or **link** to, data in other sheets and in other workbooks. Linking to a worksheet or workbook is better than retyping calculated results from another worksheet or workbook because the data values that the calculated totals depend on might change. If you reference the cells, any changes to the original values are automatically reflected in the consolidation sheet. **CASE** ▶ *Mary asks you to prepare a January sales summary sheet comparing the total U.S. revenue for the experiences sold in the month.*

STEPS

1. **Click the US Summary Jan sheet tab**

   Because the US Summary Jan sheet (which is the consolidation sheet) will contain references to the data in the other sheets, the cell pointer must reside there when you begin entering the reference.

2. **Click cell B7, click the Formulas tab, click the AutoSum button in the Function Library group, click the NY sheet tab, press and hold [Shift], click the LA sheet tab, scroll up if necessary and click cell G7, then click the Enter button ✓ on the formula bar**

   The US Summary Jan sheet becomes active, and the formula bar reads =SUM(NY:LA!G7), as shown in FIGURE 5-7. "NY:LA" references the NY and LA sheets. The exclamation point (!) is an **external reference indicator**, meaning that the cells referenced are outside the active sheet; G7 is the actual cell reference you want to total in the external sheets. The result, 7, appears in cell B7 of the US Summary Jan sheet; it is the sum of the number of Wildlife Care experiences sold and referenced in cell G7 of the NY and LA sheets. Because the Revenue data is in the column to the right of the Experiences Sold column on the NY and LA sheets, you can copy the experiences sold summary formula, with its relative addresses, into the cell that holds the revenue summary information.

3. **Drag the fill handle to copy the formula in cell B7 to cell C7, click the Auto Fill Options list arrow ⊞▾, then click the Fill Without Formatting option button**

   The result, $8,004, appears in cell C7 of the US Summary Jan sheet, showing the sum of the Wildlife Care experience revenue referenced in cell H7 of the NY and LA sheets.

4. **In the US Summary Jan sheet, with the range B7:C7 selected, drag the fill handle to fill the range B8:C10**

   You can test a consolidation reference by changing one cell value on which the formula is based and seeing if the formula result changes.

QUICK TIP
You can preview
your worksheet
with the worksheet
gridlines and column
and row headings
for printing at a later
time. On the Page
Layout tab, click the
Print check boxes
under Gridlines
and Headings in
the Sheet Options
group.

5. **Click the LA sheet tab, edit cell A6 to read Wildlife Care, then click the US Summary Jan sheet tab**

   The number of Wildlife Care experiences sold is automatically updated to 8, and the revenue is increased to $9,883, as shown in FIGURE 5-8.

6. **Save the workbook, then preview the worksheet**

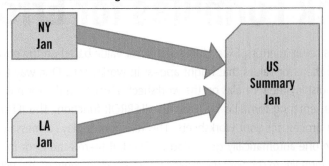

FIGURE 5-6: Consolidating data from two worksheets

FIGURE 5-7: Worksheet showing total Wildlife Care experiences sold

FIGURE 5-8: US Summary Jan worksheet with updated totals

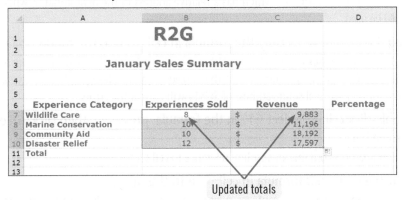

Linking data between workbooks

Just as you can link data between cells in a worksheet and between sheets in a workbook, you can link workbooks so that changes made in referenced cells in one workbook are reflected in the consolidation sheet in the other workbook. To link a single cell between workbooks, open both workbooks, select the cell to receive the linked data, type the equal sign (=), select the cell in the other workbook containing the data to be linked, then press [Enter]. Excel automatically inserts the name of the referenced workbook in the cell reference. For example, if the linked data is contained in cell C7 of the Sales worksheet in the Product workbook, the cell entry reads =[Product.xlsx]Sales!$C$7. To perform calculations, enter formulas on the consolidation sheet using cells in the supporting sheets.

Check Formulas for Errors

Learning
Outcomes
• Check for formula
errors using
IFERROR
• Display worksheet
formulas

When formulas result in errors, Excel displays an error value based on the error type. See **TABLE 5-2** for an explanation of the error values that might appear in worksheets. One way to check worksheet formulas for errors is to display the formulas on the worksheet rather than the formula results. You can also check for errors when entering formulas by using the IFERROR function. The IFERROR function simplifies the error-checking process for your worksheets. This function displays a message or value that you specify, rather than the one automatically generated by Excel, if there is an error in a formula. **CASE** *Mary asks you to use formulas to compare the experiences revenues for January. You will use the IFERROR function to help catch formula errors.*

STEPS

1. **On the US Summary Jan sheet, click cell B11, click the Formulas tab, click the AutoSum button in the Function Library group, then click the Enter button ✓ on the formula bar**
   The number of experiences sold, 40, appears in cell B11.

2. **Drag the fill handle to copy the formula in cell B11 into cell C11, click the Auto Fill options list arrow ⊞ ▾, then click the Fill Without Formatting option button**
   The experience revenue total of $56,868 appears in cell C11. You decide to enter a formula to calculate the percentage of revenue the Wildlife Care experience represents by dividing the individual experience revenue figures by the total revenue figure. To help with error checking, you decide to enter the formula using the IFERROR function.

3. **Click cell D7, click the Logical button in the Function Library group, click IFERROR, with the insertion point in the Value text box click cell C7, type /, click cell C11, press [Tab], in the Value_if_error text box type ERROR, then click OK**
   The Wildlife Care experience revenue percentage of 17.38% appears in cell D7. You want to be sure that your error message will be displayed properly, so you decide to test it by intentionally creating an error. You copy and paste the formula—which has a relative address in the denominator, where an absolute address should be used.

4. **Drag the fill handle to copy the formula in cell D7 into the range D8:D10**
   The ERROR value appears in cells D8:D10, as shown in **FIGURE 5-9**. The errors are a result of the relative address for C11 in the denominator of the copied formula. Changing the relative address of C11 in the copied formula to an absolute address of $C$11 will correct the errors.

5. **Double-click cell D7, select C11 in the formula, press [F4], then click ✓ on the formula bar**
   The formula now contains an absolute reference to cell C11.

6. **Copy the corrected formula in cell D7 into the range D8:D10**
   The experience revenue percentages now appear in all four cells, without error messages, as shown in **FIGURE 5-10**. You want to check all of your worksheet formulas by displaying them on the worksheet.

7. **Click the Show Formulas button in the Formula Auditing group**
   The formulas appear in columns B, C, and D. You want to display the formula results again. The Show Formulas button works as a toggle, turning the feature on and off with each click.

8. **Click the Show Formulas button in the Formula Auditing group**
   The formula results appear on the worksheet.

9. **Add your name to the center section of the footer, save the workbook, preview the worksheet, close the workbook, then submit the workbook to your instructor**

Analyzing Data Using Formulas

FIGURE 5-9: Worksheet with error codes

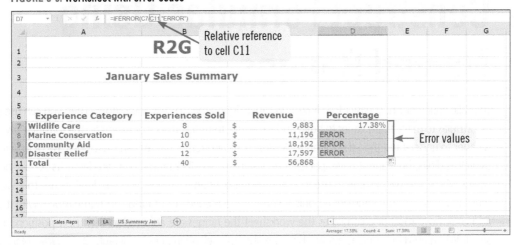

FIGURE 5-10: Worksheet with experience percentages

TABLE 5-2: Understanding error values

error value	cause of error	error value	cause of error
#DIV/0!	A number is divided by 0	#NAME?	Formula contains text error
#NA	A value in a formula is not available	#NULL!	Invalid intersection of areas
#NUM!	Invalid use of a number in a formula	#REF!	Invalid cell reference
#VALUE!	Wrong type of formula argument or operand	#####	Column is not wide enough to display data

Correcting circular references

A cell with a circular reference contains a formula that refers to its own cell location. If you accidentally enter a formula with a circular reference, a warning box opens, alerting you to the problem. Click Help to open a Help window explaining how to find the circular reference. In simple formulas, a circular reference is easy to spot. To correct it, edit the formula to remove any reference to the cell where the formula is located.

If the circular reference is intentional, you can avoid this error by enabling the iteration feature. Excel then recalculates

the formula for the number of times you specify. To enable iterative calculations, click the File tab on the Ribbon, click Options, click Formulas to view the options for calculations, click the Enable iterative calculation check box in the Calculation options group, enter the maximum number of iterations in the Maximum Iterations text box, enter the maximum amount of change between recalculation results in the Maximum Change text box, then click OK.

Construct Formulas Using Named Ranges

Learning Outcomes
- Assign names to cells
- Assign names to cell ranges
- Build formulas using names

To make your worksheet easier to follow, you can assign names to cells and ranges. Then you can use the names in formulas to make them easier to build and to reduce formula errors. For example, the formula "revenue-cost" is easier to understand than the formula "A5-A8". Cell and range names can use uppercase or lowercase letters as well as digits, but cannot have spaces. After you name a cell or range, you can define its **scope**, or the worksheets where you will be able to use it. When defining a name's scope, you can limit its use to a worksheet or make it available to the entire workbook. If you move a named cell or range, its name moves with it, and if you add or remove rows or columns to the worksheet the ranges are adjusted to their new position in the worksheet. When used in formulas, names become absolute cell references by default. **CASE** ▶ *Mary asks you to calculate the number of days before each experience departs. You will use range names to construct the formula.*

STEPS

QUICK TIP
You can also create range names by selecting a cell or range, typing a name in the Name Box, then pressing [Enter]. By default, its scope will be the workbook.

1. **Open** EX 5-2.xlsx **from the location where you store your Data Files, then save it as** EX 5-Experiences

2. **In the April Sales sheet, click cell** B4, **click the** Formulas tab **if necessary, then click the** Define Name button **in the Defined Names group**

   The New Name dialog box opens, as shown in **FIGURE 5-11**. You can give a cell that contains a date a name that will make it easier to build formulas that perform date calculations.

QUICK TIP
Because range names cannot contain spaces, underscores are often used between words to replace spaces.

3. **Type** current_date **in the Name text box, click the** Scope list arrow, **click** April Sales, **then click** OK

   The name assigned to cell B4, current_date, appears in the Name Box. Because its scope is the April Sales worksheet, the range name current_date will appear on the name list only on that worksheet.

4. **Select the range** B7:B13, **click the** Define Name button **in the Defined Names group, enter** experience_date **in the Name text box, click the** Scope list arrow, **click** April Sales, **then click** OK

   Now you can use the named cell and named range in a formula. The formula =experience_date–current_date is easier to understand than =B7-$B$4.

QUICK TIP
Named cells and ranges can be used as a navigational tool in a worksheet by selecting the name in the Name box.

5. **Click cell** C7, **type** =, **click the** Use in Formula button **in the Defined Names group, click** experience_date, **type** –, **click the** Use in Formula button, **click** current_date, **then click the** Enter button ✓ **on the formula bar**

   The number of days before the elephant conservation experience departs, 6, appears in cell C7. You can use the same formula to calculate the number of days before the other experiences depart.

6. **Drag the** fill handle **to copy the formula in cell C7 into the range** C8:C13, **then compare your formula results with those in FIGURE 5-12**

7. **Save the workbook**

Consolidating data using named ranges

You can consolidate data using named cells and ranges. For example, you might have entered team sales figures using the names team1, team2, and team3 on different sheets that you want to consolidate on one summary sheet. As you enter the summary formula you can click the Formulas tab, click the Use in Formula button in the Defined Names group, and select the cell or range name.

FIGURE 5-11: New Name dialog box

FIGURE 5-12: Worksheet with days before departure

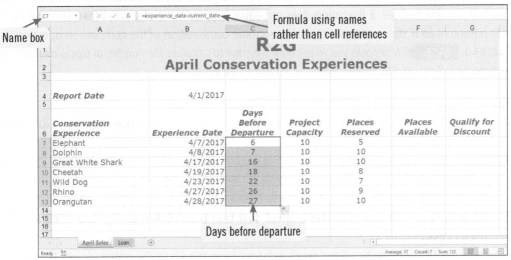

Managing workbook names

You can use the Name Manager to create, delete, and edit names in a workbook. Click the Name Manager button in the Defined Names group on the Formulas tab to open the Name Manager dialog box, shown in **FIGURE 5-13**. Click the New button to create a new named cell or range, click Delete to remove a highlighted name, and click Filter to see options for displaying specific criteria for displaying names. Clicking Edit opens the Edit Name dialog box where you can change a highlighted cell name, edit or add comments, and change the cell or cells that the name refers to on the worksheet.

FIGURE 5-13: Name Manager dialog box

Build a Logical Formula with the IF Function

Learning
Outcomes
• Build a logical
  formula using the
  IF function
• Apply comparison
  operators in a
  logical test

You can build a logical formula using an IF function. A **logical formula** makes calculations based on criteria that you create, called **stated conditions**. For example, you can build a formula to calculate bonuses based on a person's performance rating. If a person is rated a 5 (the stated condition) on a scale of 1 to 5, with 5 being the highest rating, he or she receives an additional 10% of his or her salary as a bonus; otherwise, there is no bonus. A condition that can be answered with a true or false response is called a **logical test**. The IF function has three parts, separated by commas: a condition or logical test, an action to take if the logical test or condition is true, and an action to take if the logical test or condition is false. Another way of expressing this is: IF(test_cond,do_this,else_this). Translated into an Excel IF function, the formula to calculate bonuses might look like this: IF(Rating=5,Salary*0.10,0). In other words, if the rating equals 5, multiply the salary by 0.10 (the decimal equivalent of 10%), then place the result in the selected cell; if the rating does not equal 5, place a 0 in the cell. When entering the logical test portion of an IF statement, you typically use some combination of the comparison operators listed in TABLE 5-3. **CASE** *Mary asks you to use an IF function to calculate the number of places available for each experience in April, and to display "None" if no places are available.*

STEPS

1. **Click cell F7, on the Formulas tab click the Logical button in the Function Library group, then click IF**

   The Function Arguments dialog box opens. You want the function to do the following: If the project capacity is greater than the number of places reserved, calculate the number of places that are available (capacity minus number reserved), and place the result in cell F7; otherwise, place the text "None" in the cell.

2. **With the insertion point in the Logical_test text box, click cell D7, type >, click cell E7, then press [Tab]**

   The symbol (>) represents "greater than." So far, the formula reads "If the project capacity is greater than the number of reserved places,". The next part of the function tells Excel the action to take if the capacity exceeds the reserved number of places.

QUICK TIP
You can nest IF
functions to test
several conditions in
a formula. A nested
IF function contains
IF functions inside
other IF functions to
test these multiple
conditions. The sec-
ond IF statement is
actually the value_if_
false argument of the
first IF statement.

3. **With the insertion point in the Value_if_true text box, click cell D7, type −, click cell E7, then press [Tab]**

   This part of the formula tells the program what you want it to do if the logical test is true. Continuing the translation of the formula, this part means "Subtract the number of reserved places from the project capacity." The last part of the formula tells Excel the action to take if the logical test is false (that is, if the project capacity does not exceed the number of reserved places).

4. **Type None in the Value_if_false text box, then click OK**

   The function is complete, and the result, 5 (the number of available places), appears in cell F7, as shown in FIGURE 5-14.

5. **Drag the fill handle to copy the formula in cell F7 into the range F8:F13**

   Compare your results with FIGURE 5-15.

6. **Save the workbook**

FIGURE 5-14: Worksheet with IF function

FIGURE 5-15: Worksheet showing places available

TABLE 5-3: Comparison operators

operator	meaning	operator	meaning
<	Less than	<=	Less than or equal to
>	Greater than	>=	Greater than or equal to
=	Equal to	<>	Not equal to

Build a Logical Formula with the AND Function

Learning Outcomes
- Select the AND function
- Apply logical tests using text

You can also build a logical function using the AND function. The AND function evaluates all of its arguments and **returns**, or displays, TRUE if every logical test in the formula is true. The AND function returns a value of FALSE if one or more of its logical tests is false. The AND function arguments can include text, numbers, or cell references. **CASE** ▸ *Mary wants you to analyze the sales data to find experiences that qualify for discounting. You will use the AND function to check for experiences with places available and that depart within 21 days.*

STEPS

TROUBLE
If you get a formula error, check to be sure that you typed the quotation marks around None.

1. **Click cell G7, click the Logical button in the Function Library group, then click AND**

   The Function Arguments dialog box opens. You want the function to evaluate the discount qualification as follows: There must be places available, and the experience must depart within 21 days.

2. **With the insertion point in the Logical1 text box, click cell F7, type < >, type "None", then press [Tab]**

   The symbol (<>) represents "not equal to." So far, the formula reads "If the number of places available is not equal to None"—in other words, if it is an integer. The next logical test checks the number of days before the experience departs.

QUICK TIP
Functions can be placed inside of an IF function. For example, the formula in cell G7 could be replaced by the formula =IF(AND(F7<> "None", C7<21), "TRUE", "FALSE")

3. **With the insertion point in the Logical2 text box, click cell C7, type <21, then click OK**

   The function is complete, and the result, TRUE, appears in cell G7, as shown in **FIGURE 5-16**.

4. **Drag the fill handle to copy the formula in cell G7 into the range G8:G13**

   Compare your results with **FIGURE 5-17**.

QUICK TIP
You can fit your worksheet on one page to print by clicking the Page Layout tab, clicking the Width list arrow in the Scale to Fit group, then clicking 1 page.

5. **Add your name to the center of the footer, save the workbook, then preview the worksheet**

Using the OR and NOT logical functions

The OR logical function has the same syntax as the AND function, but rather than returning TRUE if every argument is true, the OR function will return TRUE if any of its arguments are true. It will only return FALSE if all of its arguments are false. The NOT logical function reverses the value of its argument. For example NOT(TRUE) reverses its argument of TRUE and returns FALSE. This can be used in a worksheet to ensure that a cell is not equal to a particular value. See **TABLE 5-4** for examples of the AND, OR, and NOT functions.

TABLE 5-4: Examples of AND, OR, and NOT functions with cell values A1=10 and B1=20

function	formula	result
AND	=AND(A1>5,B1>25)	FALSE
OR	=OR(A1>5,B1>25)	TRUE
NOT	=NOT(A1=0)	TRUE

FIGURE 5-16: Worksheet with AND function

FIGURE 5-17: Worksheet with discount status evaluated

Calculate Payments with the PMT Function

Learning Outcomes
- Calculate monthly payments using the PMT function
- Edit the PMT function to display payments as a positive value

PMT is a financial function that calculates the periodic payment amount for money borrowed. For example, if you want to borrow money to buy a car, and you know the principal amount, interest rate, and loan term, the PMT function can calculate your monthly payment. See **FIGURE 5-18** for an illustration of a PMT function that calculates the monthly payment for a $20,000 car loan at 6.5% interest over 5 years. **CASE** *For several months, R2G's United States region has been discussing opening a new branch in San Francisco. Mary has obtained quotes from three different lenders on borrowing $500,000 to begin the expansion. She obtained loan quotes from a commercial bank, a venture capitalist, and an investment banker. She wants you to summarize the information using the Excel PMT function.*

STEPS

1. **Click the** Loan sheet tab, **click cell** F5, **click the** Formulas tab, **click the** Financial button **in the Function Library group, scroll down the list of functions, then click** PMT

2. **With the insertion point in the Rate text box, click cell** D5 **on the worksheet, type** /12, **then press** [Tab]

   You must divide the annual interest by 12 because you are calculating monthly, not annual, payments. You need to be consistent about the units you use for rate and nper. If you express nper as the number of monthly payments, then you must express the interest rate as a monthly rate.

QUICK TIP

The Fv and Type arguments are optional: Fv is the future value, or the total amount you want to obtain after all payments. If you omit it, Excel assumes you want to pay off the loan completely, so the default Fv is 0. Type indicates when the payments are made; 0 is the end of the period, and 1 is the beginning of the period. The default is the end of the period.

3. **With the insertion point in the Nper text box click cell** E5, **click the** Pv text box, **click cell** B5, **then click** OK

   The payment of ($5,242.39) in cell F5 appears in red, indicating that it is a negative amount. Excel displays the result of a PMT function as a negative value to reflect the negative cash flow the loan represents to the borrower. To show the monthly payment as a positive number, you can place a minus sign in front of the Pv cell reference in the function.

4. **Double-click cell** F5, **edit it to read** =PMT(D5/12,E5,-B5), **then click the** Enter button ☑ **on the formula bar**

   A positive value of $5,242.39 now appears in cell F5, as shown in **FIGURE 5-19**. You can use the same formula to generate the monthly payments for the other loans.

5. **With cell** F5 **selected, drag the** fill handle **to fill the range** F6:F7

   A monthly payment of $9,424.17 for the venture capitalist loan appears in cell F6. A monthly payment of $14,996.68 for the investment banker loan appears in cell F7. The loans with shorter terms have much higher monthly payments. But you will not know the entire financial picture until you calculate the total payments and total interest for each lender.

QUICK TIP

You can use the keyboard shortcut of [Ctrl][Enter] rather than clicking the Enter button. This enters the formula and leaves the cell selected.

6. **Click cell** G5, **type** =, **click cell** E5, **type** *, **click cell** F5, **press** [Tab], **in cell H5 type** =, **click cell** G5, **type** –, **click cell** B5, **then click** ☑

7. **Copy the formulas in cells** G5:H5 **into the range** G6:H7, **then click cell** A1

   You can experiment with different interest rates, loan amounts, or terms for any one of the lenders; the PMT function generates a new set of values automatically.

8. **Add your name to the center section of the footer, save the workbook, preview the worksheet, submit the workbook to your instructor, close the workbook, then exit Excel**

   Your worksheet appears as shown in **FIGURE 5-20**.

FIGURE 5-18: Example of PMT function for car loan

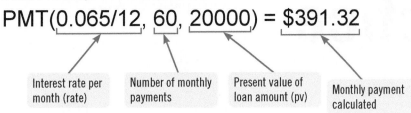

PMT(0.065/12, 60, 20000) = $391.32

Interest rate per month (rate)

Number of monthly payments

Present value of loan amount (pv)

Monthly payment calculated

FIGURE 5-19: PMT function calculating monthly loan payment

F5   fx   =PMT(D5/12,E5,-B5)

R2G
Expansion Loan Summary

Lender	Loan Amount	Term (Years)	Interest Rate	Term (Months)	Monthly Payment	Total Payments	Total Interest
Commercial Bank	$500,000	10	4.75%	120	$5,242.39		
Venture Capitalist	$500,000	5	4.95%	60			
Investment Banker	$500,000	3	5.05%	36			

Minus sign before present value displays payment as a positive amount

FIGURE 5-20: Completed worksheet

R2G
Expansion Loan Summary

Lender	Loan Amount	Term (Years)	Interest Rate	Term (Months)	Monthly Payment	Total Payments	Total Interest
Commercial Bank	$500,000	10	4.75%	120	$5,242.39	$629,086.46	$129,086.46
Venture Capitalist	$500,000	5	4.95%	60	$9,424.17	$565,450.05	$65,450.05
Investment Banker	$500,000	3	5.05%	36	$14,996.68	$539,880.32	$39,880.32

Calculating future value with the FV function

You can use the FV (Future Value) function to determine the amount of money a given monthly investment will amount to, at a given interest rate, after a given number of payment periods. The syntax is similar to that of the PMT function: FV(rate,nper,pmt,pv,type). The rate is the interest paid by the financial institution, the nper is the number of periods, and the pmt is the amount that you deposit. For example, suppose you want to invest $1,000 every month for the next 12 months into an account that pays 2% a year, and you want to know how much you will have at the end of 12 months (that is, its future value). You enter the function FV(.02/12,12,-1000), and Excel returns the value $12,110.61 as the future value of your investment. As with the PMT function, the units for the rate and nper must be consistent.

Practice

Concepts Review

FIGURE 5-21

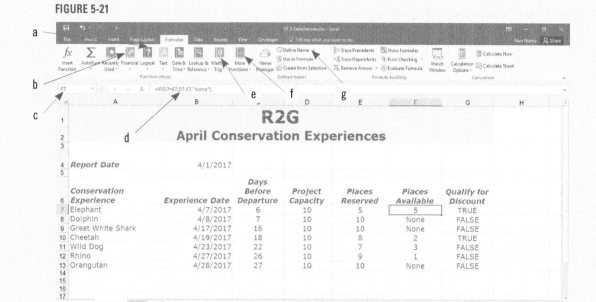

1. Which element do you click to name a cell or range and define its scope?
2. Which element do you click to add a statistical function to a worksheet?
3. Which element points to a logical formula?
4. Which element points to the area where the name of a selected cell or range appears?
5. Which element do you click to add a SUMIF function to a worksheet?
6. Which element do you click to insert a PMT function into a worksheet?
7. Which element do you click to add an IF function to a worksheet?

Match each term with the statement that best describes it.

8. FV
9. PV
10. SUMIF
11. PROPER
12. test_cond

a. Function used to change the first letter of a string to uppercase
b. Function used to determine the future amount of an investment
c. Part of the PMT function that represents the loan amount
d. Part of the IF function that the conditions are stated in
e. Function used to conditionally total cells

Select the best answer from the list of choices.

13. To express conditions such as less than or equal to, you can use a:
    a. Text formula.
    b. Comparison operator.
    c. PMT function.
    d. Statistical function.
14. When you enter the rate and nper arguments in a PMT function, you must:
    a. Be consistent in the units used.
    b. Multiply both units by 12.
    c. Divide both values by 12.
    d. Always use annual units.

15. Which of the following is an external reference indicator in a formula?

a. &

c. !

b. :

d. =

16. Which of the following statements is false?

a. When used in formulas, names become relative cell references by default.

b. Names cannot contain spaces.

c. Named ranges make formulas easier to build.

d. If you move a named cell or range, its name moves with it.

17. Which function joins text strings into one text string?

a. Proper

c. Combine

b. Join

d. Concatenate

18. When using text in logical tests, the text must be enclosed in:

a. " "

c. !

b. ( )

d. < >

Skills Review

1. Format data using text functions.

a. Start Excel, open EX 5-3.xlsx from the location where you store your Data Files, then save it as **EX 5-North Systems**.

b. On the Managers worksheet, select cell B4 and use the Flash Fill button on the Data tab to enter the names into column B.

c. In cell D2, use a text function to convert the first letter of the department in cell C2 to uppercase, then copy the formula in cell D2 into the range D3:D9.

d. In cell E2, use a text function to convert all letters of the department in cell C2 to uppercase, then copy the formula in cell E2 into the range E3:E9. Widen column E to fit the uppercase entries.

e. In cell F2, use a text function to convert all letters of the department in cell C2 to lowercase, then copy the formula in cell F2 into the range F3:F9.

f. In cell G2, use a text function to substitute "IT" for "operations" if that text exists in cell F2. (*Hint*: In the Function Arguments dialog box, Text is F2, Old_text is "operations", and New_text is "IT".) Copy the formula in cell G2 into the range G3:G9 to change any cells containing "operations" to "IT."

g. Save your work, then enter your name in the worksheet footer. Switch back to Normal view, then compare your screen to **FIGURE 5-22**.

FIGURE 5-22

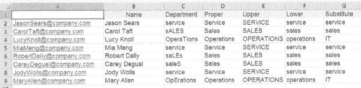

	A	B	C	D	E	F	G
1		Name	Department	Proper	Upper	Lower	Substitute
2	JasonSears@company.com	Jason Sears	service	Service	SERVICE	service	service
3	CarolTaft@company.com	Carol Taft	sALES	Sales	SALES	sales	sales
4	LucyKnoll@company.com	Lucy Knoll	OperaTions	Operations	OPERATIONS	operations	IT
5	MiaMeng@company.com	Mia Meng	service	Service	SERVICE	service	service
6	RobertDally@company.com	Robert Dally	saLEs	Sales	SALES	sales	sales
7	CareyDegual@company.com	Carey Degual	saleS	Sales	SALES	sales	sales
8	JodyWolls@company.com	Jody Wolls	service	Service	SERVICE	service	service
9	MaryAllen@company.com	Mary Allen	OpErations	Operations	OPERATIONS	operations	IT
10							

h. Display the formulas in the worksheet.

i. Redisplay the formula results.

2. Sum a data range based on conditions.

a. Make the Service sheet active.

b. In cell B20, use the COUNTIF function to count the number of employees with a rating of 5.

c. In cell B21, use the AVERAGEIF function to average the salaries of those with a rating of 5.

d. In cell B22, enter the SUMIF function that totals the salaries of employees with a rating of 5.

e. Format cells B21 and B22 with the Number format using commas and no decimals. Save your work, then compare your formula results to **FIGURE 5-23**.

FIGURE 5-23

18	Department Statistics	
19	Top Rating	
20	Number	4
21	Average Salary	58,110
22	Total Salary	232,440
23		

Skills Review (continued)

3. Consolidate data using a formula.

a. Make the Summary sheet active.

b. In cell B4, use the AutoSum function to total cell F15 on the Service and Accounting sheets.

c. Format cell B4 with the Accounting Number format with two decimal places.

d. Enter your name in the worksheet footer, then save your work. Return to Normal view, then compare your screen to **FIGURE 5-24**.

e. Display the formula in the worksheet, then redisplay the formula results in the worksheet.

4. Check formulas for errors.

a. Make the Service sheet active.

b. In cell I6, use the IFERROR function to display "ERROR" in the event that the formula F6/F15 results in a formula error. (*Note:* This formula will generate an intentional error after the next step, which you will correct in a moment.)

c. Copy the formula in cell I6 into the range I7:I14.

d. Correct the formula in cell I6 by making the denominator, F15, an absolute address.

e. Copy the new formula in cell I6 into the range I7:I14, then save your work.

5. Construct formulas using named ranges.

a. On the Service sheet, name the range C6:C14 **review_date**, and limit the scope of the name to the Service worksheet.

b. In cell E6, enter the formula **=review_date+183**, using the Use in Formula button to enter the cell name.

c. Copy the formula in cell E6 into the range E7:E14.

d. Use the Name Manager to add a comment of **Date of last review** to the review_date name. (*Hint:* In the Name Manager dialog box, click the review_date name, then click Edit to enter the comment.) Widen the worksheet columns to display all of the data as necessary, then save your work.

6. Build a logical formula with the IF function.

a. In cell G6, use the Function Arguments dialog box to enter the formula **=IF(D6=5,F6*0.05,0)**.

b. Copy the formula in cell G6 into the range G7:G14.

c. In cell G15, use AutoSum to total the range G6:G14.

d. Save your work.

7. Build a logical formula with the AND function.

a. In cell H6, use the Function Arguments dialog box to enter the formula **=AND(G6>0,B6>6)**.

b. Copy the formula in cell H6 into the range H7:H14.

c. Enter your name in the footers of the Service and Accounting sheets, save your work, then return to Normal view and compare your Service worksheet to **FIGURE 5-25**.

FIGURE 5-24

	A	B
1	**Salary Summary**	
2		
3		Salary
4	TOTAL	$ 852,035.00
5		

FIGURE 5-25

	A	B	C	D	E	F	G	H	I
1					*Service Department*				
2					*Bonus Pay*				
3									
4									
5	Last Name	Professional Development Hours	Review Date	Rating	Next Review	Salary	Bonus	Pay Bonus	Percentage of Total
6	Boady	5	1/7/2017	5	7/9/2017	$ 59,740.00	$2,987.00	FALSE	13.73%
7	Cane	9	4/1/2017	4	10/1/2017	66,800.00	$0.00	FALSE	15.35%
8	Dugal	1	6/1/2017	4	12/1/2017	33,400.00	$0.00	FALSE	7.67%
9	Hennely	7	4/1/2017	5	10/1/2017	45,500.00	$2,275.00	TRUE	10.45%
10	Krones	10	3/1/2017	4	8/31/2017	37,500.00	$0.00	FALSE	8.62%
11	Malone	4	5/15/2017	3	11/14/2017	36,500.00	$0.00	FALSE	8.39%
12	Mercy	4	6/1/2017	5	12/1/2017	57,500.00	$2,875.00	FALSE	13.21%
13	Stone	6	8/1/2017	3	1/31/2018	28,600.00	$0.00	FALSE	6.57%
14	Storey	8	7/23/2017	5	1/22/2018	69,700.00	$3,485.00	TRUE	16.01%
15	Totals					$ 435,240.00	$11,622.00		

Skills Review (continued)

8. Calculate payments with the PMT function.

a. Make the Loan sheet active.

b. In cell B9, determine the monthly payment using the loan information shown: Use the Function Arguments dialog box to enter the formula **=PMT(B5/12,B6,-B4)**.

c. In cell B10, enter a formula that multiplies the number of payments by the monthly payment.

d. In cell B11, enter the formula that subtracts the loan amount from the total payment amount, then compare your screen to **FIGURE 5-26**.

e. Enter your name in the worksheet footer, save the workbook, then submit your workbook to your instructor.

f. Close the workbook, then exit Excel.

FIGURE 5-26

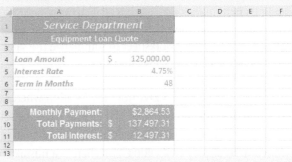

Independent Challenge 1

As the accounting manager of Ace Floors, a carpet and flooring company, you are reviewing the accounts payable information for your advertising accounts and prioritizing the overdue invoices for your collections service. You will analyze the invoices and use logical functions to emphasize priority accounts.

a. Start Excel, open EX 5-4.xlsx from the location where you store your Data Files, then save it as **EX 5-Ace**.

b. Name the range B7:B13 **invoice_date**, and give the name a scope of the accounts payable worksheet.

c. Name the cell B4 **current_date**, and give the name a scope of the accounts payable worksheet.

d. Enter a formula using the named range invoice_date in cell E7 that calculates the invoice due date by adding 30 to the invoice date.

e. Copy the formula in cell E7 to the range E8:E13.

f. In cell F7, enter a formula using the named range invoice_date and the named cell current_date that calculates the invoice age by subtracting the invoice date from the current date.

g. Copy the formula in cell F7 to the range F8:F13.

h. In cell G7, enter an IF function that calculates the number of days an invoice is overdue, assuming that an invoice must be paid in 30 days. (*Hint*: The Logical_test should check to see if the age of the invoice is greater than 30, the Value_if_true should calculate the current date minus the invoice due date, and the Value_if_false should be 0.) Copy the IF function into the range G8:G13.

i. In cell H7, enter an AND function to prioritize the overdue invoices that are more than $1,000 for collection services. (*Hint*: The Logical1 condition should check to see if the number of days overdue is more than 0, and the Logical2 condition should check if the amount is more than 1,000.) Copy the AND function into the range H8:H13.

j. Use the Name Manager to name the range H7:H13 **Priority** and give the name a scope of the accounts payable worksheet. (*Hint*: In the Name Manager dialog box, click New to enter the range name.)

k. Enter your name in the worksheet footer, save the workbook, preview the worksheet, then submit the workbook to your instructor.

l. Close the workbook, then exit Excel.

Excel 2016

Independent Challenge 2

You are an auditor with a certified public accounting firm. Boston Paper, an online seller of office products, has contacted you to audit its first-quarter sales records. The management is considering expanding and needs its sales records audited to prepare the business plan. Specifically, they want to show what percent of annual sales each category represents. You will use a formula on a summary worksheet to summarize the sales for January, February, and March and to calculate the overall first-quarter percentage of the sales categories.

a. Start Excel, open EX 5-5.xlsx from the location where you store your Data Files, then save it as **EX 5-Paper**.

b. In cell B10 of the Jan, Feb, and Mar sheets, enter the formulas to calculate the sales totals for the month.

c. For each month, in cell C5, create a formula calculating the percent of sales for the Equipment sales category. Use a function to display "INCORRECT" if there is a mistake in the formula. Verify that the percent appears with two decimal places. Copy this formula as necessary to complete the % of sales for all sales categories on all sheets. If any cells display "INCORRECT", fix the formulas in those cells.

d. In column B of the Summary sheet, use formulas to total the sales categories for the Jan, Feb, and Mar worksheets.

e. Enter the formula to calculate the first quarter sales total in cell B10 using the sales totals on the Jan, Feb, and Mar worksheets.

f. Calculate the percent of each sales category on the Summary sheet. Use a function to display "MISCALCULATION" if there is a mistake in the formula. Copy this formula as necessary. If any cells display "MISCALCULATION", fix the formulas in those cells.

g. Enter your name in the Summary worksheet footer, save the workbook, preview the worksheet, then submit it to your instructor.

FIGURE 5-27

	A	B	C	D	E
1	equipment	paper	stationery	ink	toner
2	EQUIPMENT	PAPER	STATIONERY	INK	TONER
3					

h. On the Products sheet, separate the product list in cell A1 into separate columns of text data. (*Hint*: With cell A1 as the active cell, use the Text to Columns button in the Data Tools group of the Data tab. The products are delimited with commas.) Use the second row to display the products in uppercase, as shown in **FIGURE 5-27**. Widen the columns as necessary.

i. Enter your name in the Products worksheet footer, save the workbook, preview the worksheet, then submit the workbook to your instructor.

Independent Challenge 3

As the owner of GWW, an advertising firm, you are planning to expand your business. Because you will have to purchase additional equipment and hire a new part-time accounts manager, you decide to take out a $100,000 loan to finance your expansion expenses. You check three loan sources: the Small Business Administration (SBA), your local bank, and a consortium of investors. The SBA will lend you the money at 4.5% interest, but you have to pay it off in 4 years. The local bank offers you the loan at 5.75% interest over 5 years. The consortium offers you a 8.25% loan, and they require you to pay it back in 2 years. To analyze all three loan options, you decide to build a loan summary worksheet. Using the loan terms provided, build a worksheet summarizing your options.

a. Start Excel, open a new workbook, save it as **EX 5-Options**, then rename Sheet1 **Loan Summary**.

b. Using **FIGURE 5-28** as a guide, enter labels and worksheet data for the three loan sources in columns A through D. Use the formatting of your choice.

FIGURE 5-28

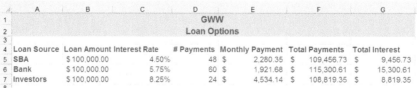

	A	B	C	D	E	F	G
1				GWW			
2				Loan Options			
3							
4	Loan Source	Loan Amount	Interest Rate	# Payments	Monthly Payment	Total Payments	Total Interest
5	SBA	$100,000.00	4.50%	48	$ 2,280.35	$ 109,456.73	$ 9,456.73
6	Bank	$100,000.00	5.75%	60	$ 1,921.68	$ 115,300.61	$ 15,300.61
7	Investors	$100,000.00	8.25%	24	$ 4,534.14	$ 108,819.35	$ 8,819.35
8							

Independent Challenge 3 (continued)

c. Enter the monthly payment formula for your first loan source (making sure to show the payment as a positive amount), copy the formula as appropriate, then name the range containing the monthly payment formulas **Monthly_Payment** with a scope of the workbook.

d. Name the cell range containing the number of payments **Number_Payments** with the scope of the workbook.

e. Enter the formula for total payments for your first loan source using the named ranges Monthly_Payment and Number_Payments, then copy the formula as necessary.

f. Name the cell range containing the formulas for Total payments **Total_Payments**. Name the cell range containing the loan amounts **Loan_Amount**. Each name should have the workbook as its scope.

g. Enter the formula for total interest for your first loan source using the named ranges Total_Payments and Loan_Amount, then copy the formula as necessary.

h. Format the worksheet using appropriate formatting, then enter your name in the worksheet footer.

i. Save the workbook, preview the worksheet and change it to landscape orientation on a single page, then submit the workbook to your instructor.

j. Close the workbook, then exit Excel.

Independent Challenge 4: Explore

As the physical therapist at NE Rehab, you are using a weekly worksheet to log and analyze the training for each of your patients. As part of this therapy, you record daily walking, biking, swimming, and weight training data and analyze it on a weekly basis.

a. Start Excel, open EX 5-6.xlsx from the location where you store your Data Files, then save it as **EX 5-Activity**.

b. Use SUMIF functions in cells G5:G8 to calculate the total minutes spent on each corresponding activity in cells F5:F8.

c. Use AVERAGEIF functions in cells H5:H8 to calculate the average number of minutes spent on each corresponding activity in cells F5:F8.

d. Use COUNTIF functions in cells I5:I8 to calculate the number of times each activity in cells F5:F8 was performed. (*Hint*: The Range of cells to count is $B$4:$B$15.)

e. Use the SUMIFS function in cell G9 to calculate the total number of minutes spent walking outdoors.

f. Use the AVERAGEIFS function in cell H9 to calculate the average number of minutes spent walking outdoors.

g. Use the COUNTIFS function in cell I9 to calculate the number of days spent walking outdoors. Compare your worksheet to FIGURE 5-29 and adjust your cell formatting as needed to match the figure.

h. Enter your name in the worksheet footer, save the workbook, preview the worksheet, then submit it to your instructor.

i. Close the workbook, then exit Excel.

FIGURE 5-29

	A	B	C	D	E	F	G	H	I
1					NE Rehab				
2	Client Name:	Karl Logan							
3	Date	Activity	Minutes	Location			Week of January 2nd		
4						Activity	Total Minutes	Average Minutes	Number of Workouts
5	1/2/2017	Walk	40	Gym		Walk	172	43.00	4
6	1/2/2017	Swim	30	Aquatics Center		Swim	125	41.67	3
7	1/3/2017	Walk	50	Outdoors		Bike	80	26.67	3
8	1/3/2017	Bike	25	Outdoors		Weights	60	30.00	2
9	1/4/2017	Walk	42	Outdoors		Walk Outdoors	92	46	2
10	1/4/2017	Weights	30	Gym					
11	1/5/2017	Swim	50	Aquatics Center					
12	1/6/2017	Weights	30	Gym					
13	1/6/2017	Bike	30	Outdoors					
14	1/7/2017	Walk	40	Gym					
15	1/7/2017	Swim	45	Aquatics Center					
16	1/8/2017	Bike	25	Gym					

Visual Workshop

Open EX 5-7.xlsx from the location where you store your Data Files, then save it as **EX 5-Bonus**. Create the worksheet shown in **FIGURE 5-30** using the data in columns B, C, and D along with the following criteria:

- The employee is eligible for a bonus if:
  - The employee has sales that exceed the sales quota.
    AND
  - The employee has a performance rating of seven or higher.
- If the employee is eligible for a bonus, the bonus amount is calculated as three percent of the sales amount. Otherwise the bonus amount is 0. (*Hint*: Use an AND formula to determine if a person is eligible for a bonus, and use an IF formula to check eligibility and to enter the bonus amount.) Enter your name in the worksheet footer, save the workbook, preview the worksheet, then submit the worksheet to your instructor.

FIGURE 5-30

	A	B	C	D	E	F	G
1			Fitness Unlimited				
2			Bonus Pay Summary				
3	Last Name	Quota	Sales	Performance Rating	Eligible	Bonus Amount	
4	Andrews	$145,000	$157,557	7	TRUE	$4,727	
5	Lee	$78,587	$91,588	3	FALSE	$0	
6	Atkinson	$113,984	$125,474	9	TRUE	$3,764	
7	Halley	$135,977	$187,255	5	FALSE	$0	
8	Pratt	$187,900	$151,228	8	FALSE	$0	
9	Balla	$128,744	$152,774	5	FALSE	$0	
10	Cruz	$129,855	$160,224	7	TRUE	$4,807	
11	Yanck	$94,000	$87,224	3	FALSE	$0	
12	Green	$79,500	$86,700	9	TRUE	$2,601	
13							

Glossary

3-D reference A worksheet reference that uses values on other sheets or workbooks, effectively creating another dimension to a workbook.

Absolute cell reference In a formula, a cell address that refers to a specific cell and does not change when you copy the formula; indicated by a dollar sign before the column letter and/or row number. *See also* Relative cell reference.

Active The currently available document, program, or object; on the taskbar, when more than one program is open, the button for the active program appears slightly lighter.

Active cell The cell in which you are currently working.

Alignment The placement of cell contents in relation to a cell's edges; for example, left-aligned, centered, or right-aligned.

Argument Information necessary for a formula or function to calculate an answer.

Arithmetic operators In a formula, symbols that perform mathematical calculations, such as addition (+), subtraction (–), multiplication (*), division (/), or exponentiation (^).

AutoFill Feature activated by dragging the fill handle; copies a cell's contents or continues a series of entries into adjacent cells.

AutoFill Options button Button that appears after using the fill handle to copy cell contents; enables you to choose to fill cells with specific elements (such as formatting) of the copied cell if desired.

AutoFit A feature that automatically adjusts the width of a column or the height of a row to accommodate its widest or tallest entry.

Backstage view View that appears when File tab is clicked. The navigation bar on the left side contains commands to perform actions common to most Office programs, such as opening a file, saving a file, and closing the file.

Backward-compatible Software feature that enables documents saved in an older version of a program to be opened in a newer version of the program.

Business Intelligence tools Excel features for gathering and analyzing data to answer sophisticated business questions.

Calculation operators Symbols in a formula that indicate what type of calculation to perform on the cells, ranges, or values.

Category axis Horizontal axis in a chart, usually containing the names of data categories; in a 2-dimensional chart, also known as the x-axis.

Cell The intersection of a column and a row in a worksheet or table.

Cell address The location of a cell, expressed by cell coordinates; for example, the cell address of the cell in column A, row 1 is A1.

Cell pointer Dark rectangle that outlines the active cell.

Cell styles Predesigned combinations of formats based on themes that can be applied to selected cells to enhance the look of a worksheet.

Chart sheet A separate sheet in a workbook that contains only a chart, which is linked to the workbook data.

Charts Pictorial representations of worksheet data that make it easier to see patterns, trends, and relationships; *also called* graphs.

Clip art A graphic image, such as a corporate logo, a picture, or a photo, that can be inserted into a document.

Clipboard A temporary Windows storage area that holds the selections you copy or cut.

Cloud computing Work done in a virtual environment using data, applications, and resources stored on servers and accessed over the Internet or a company's internal network rather than on users' computers.

Column heading Box that appears above each column in a worksheet; identifies the column letter, such as A, B, etc.

Combination chart Two charts in one, such as a column chart combined with a line chart, that together graph related but dissimilar data.

Comparison operators In a formula, symbols that compare values for the purpose of true/false results.

Compatibility The ability of different programs to work together and exchange data.

Complex formula A formula that uses more than one arithmetic operator.

Conditional formatting A type of cell formatting that changes based on the cell's value or the outcome of a formula.

Consolidate To combine data on multiple worksheets and display the result on another worksheet.

Contextual tab A tab that is displayed only when a specific task can be performed: they appear in an accent color and close when no longer needed.

Data marker A graphical representation of a data point in a chart, such as a bar or column.

Data point Individual piece of data plotted in a chart.

Data series The selected range in a worksheet whose related data points Excel converts into a chart.

Delimiter A separator such as a space, comma, or semicolon between elements in imported data.

Dialog box launcher An icon you can click to open a dialog box or task pane from which to choose related commands.

Document window Most of the screen in any given program, where you create a document, slide, or worksheet.

Edit To make a change to the contents of an active cell.

Electronic spreadsheet A computer program used to perform calculations and analyze and present numeric data.

Embedded chart A chart displayed as an object in a worksheet.

Exploding Visually pulling a slice of a pie chart away from the whole pie chart in order to add emphasis to the pie slice.

External reference indicator The exclamation point (!) used in a formula to indicate that a referenced cell is outside the active sheet.

File A stored collection of data.

Flash Fill An Excel feature that automatically fills in column or row data based on calculations you enter.

Font The typeface or design of a set of characters (letters, numbers, symbols, and punctuation marks).

Font size The size of characters, measured in units called points.

Font style Format such as bold, italic, and underlining that can be applied to change the way characters look in a worksheet or chart.

Format The appearance of a cell and its contents, including font, font styles, font color, fill color, borders, and shading. *See also* Number format.

Formula A set of instructions used to perform one or more numeric calculations, such as adding, multiplying, or averaging, on values or cells.

Formula bar The area above the worksheet grid where you enter or edit data in the active cell.

Formula prefix An arithmetic symbol, such as the equal sign (=), used to start a formula.

Function A special, predefined formula that provides a shortcut for a commonly used or complex calculation, such as SUM (for calculating a sum) or FV (for calculating the future value of an investment).

Gallery A visual collection of choices you can browse through to make a selection. Often available with Live Preview.

Gridlines Evenly spaced horizontal and/or vertical lines used in a worksheet or chart to make it easier to read.

Groups Each tab on the Ribbon is arranged into groups to make features easy to find.

Insertion point A blinking vertical line that appears when you click in the formula bar or in an active cell; indicates where new text will be inserted.

Integrate To incorporate a document and parts of a document created in one program into another program; for example, to incorporate an Excel chart into a PowerPoint slide, or an Access table into a Word document.

Interface The look and feel of a program; for example, the appearance of commands and the way they are organized in the program window.

Labels Descriptive text or other information that identifies data in rows, columns, or charts, but is not included in calculations.

Landscape Page orientation in which the contents of a page span the length of a page rather than its width, making the page wider than it is tall.

Launch To open or start a program on your computer.

Legend In a chart, information that identifies how data is represented by colors or patterns.

Linking The dynamic referencing of data in the same or in other workbooks, so that when data in the other location is changed, the references in the current location are automatically updated.

Live Preview A feature that lets you point to a choice in a gallery or palette and see the results in the document without actually clicking the choice.

Logical formula A formula with calculations that are based on stated conditions.

Logical test The first part of an IF function; if the logical test is true, then the second part of the function is applied; if it is false, then the third part of the function is applied.

Major gridlines In a chart, the gridlines that represent the values at the tick marks on the value axis.

Minor gridlines In a chart, the gridlines that represent the values between the tick marks on the value axis.

Mixed reference Cell reference that combines both absolute and relative cell addressing.

Mode indicator An area on the left end of the status bar that indicates the program's status. For example, when you are changing the contents of a cell, the word 'Edit' appears in the mode indicator.

Name box Box to the left of the formula bar that shows the cell reference or name of the active cell.

Navigate To move around in a worksheet; for example, you can use the arrow keys on the keyboard to navigate from cell to cell, or press [Page Up] or [Page Down] to move one screen at a time.

Normal view Default worksheet view that shows the worksheet without features such as headers and footers; ideal for creating and editing a worksheet, but may not be detailed enough when formatting a document.

Number format A format applied to values to express numeric concepts, such as currency, date, and percentage.

Object Independent element on a worksheet (such as a chart or graphic) that is not located in a specific cell or range; can be moved and resized and displays handles when selected.

OneDrive An online storage and file sharing service. Access to OneDrive is through a Microsoft account.

Online collaboration The ability to incorporate feedback or share information across the Internet or a company network or intranet.

Order of precedence Rules that determine the order in which operations are performed within a formula containing more than one arithmetic operator.

Page In OneNote, a workspace for inserting notes and other content, similar to a page in a physical notebook.

Page Break Preview A worksheet view that displays a reduced view of each page in your worksheet, along with page break indicators that you can drag to include more or less information on a page.

Page Layout view Provides an accurate view of how a worksheet will look when printed, including headers and footers.

Paste Options button Button that appears onscreen after pasting content; enables you to choose to paste only specific elements of the copied selection, such as the formatting or values, if desired.

Plot area In a chart, the area inside the horizontal and vertical axes.

Point A unit of measure used for font size and row height. One point is equal to 1/72nd of an inch.

Portrait Page orientation in which the contents of a page span the width of a page, so the page is taller than it is wide.

Previewing Prior to printing, seeing onscreen exactly how the printed document will look.

Print area The portion of a worksheet that will be printed; can be defined by selecting a range and then using the Print Area button on the Page Layout tab.

Quick Access toolbar A small toolbar on the left side of a Microsoft application program window's title bar, containing icons that you click to quickly perform common actions, such as saving a file.

Quick Analysis tool An icon that is displayed below and to the right of a range that lets you easily create charts and other elements.

Range A selection of two or more cells, such as B5:B14.

Reference operators In a formula, symbols which enable you to use ranges in calculations.

Relative cell reference In a formula, a cell address that refers to a cell's location in relation to the cell containing the formula and that automatically changes to reflect the new location when the formula is copied or moved; default type of referencing used in Excel worksheets. *See also* Absolute cell reference.

Return In a function, to display a result.

Ribbon Appears beneath the title bar in every Office program window, and displays commands you're likely to need for the current task.

Scope In a named cell or range, the worksheet(s) in which the name can be used.

Screen capture An electronic snapshot of your screen, as if you took a picture of it with a camera, which you can paste into a document.

Scroll bars Bars on the right edge (vertical scroll bar) and bottom edge (horizontal scroll bar) of the document window that allow you to move around in a document that is too large to fit on the screen at once.

Secondary axis In a combination chart, an additional axis that supplies the scale for one of the chart types used.

Sheet tab scrolling buttons Allow you to navigate to additional sheet tabs when available; located to the left of the sheet tabs.

Sheet tabs Identify the sheets in a workbook and let you switch between sheets; located below the worksheet grid.

Sizing handles Small series of dots at the corners and edges of a chart indicating that the chart is selected; drag to resize the chart.

SmartArt graphics Predesigned diagram types for the following types of data: List, Process, Cycle, Hierarchy, Relationship, Matrix, and Pyramid.

Sparkline A quick, simple chart located within a cell that serves as a visual indicator of data trends.

Stated conditions In a logical formula, criteria you create.

Status bar Bar at the bottom of the Excel window that provides a brief description about the active command or task in progress.

Suite A group of programs that are bundled together and share a similar interface, making it easy to transfer skills and program content among them.

Table An organized collection of rows and columns of similarly structured data on a worksheet.

Table styles Predesigned formatting that can be applied to a range of cells or even to an entire worksheet; especially useful for those ranges with labels in the left column and top row, and totals in the bottom row or right column. *See also* Table.

Tabs Organizational unit used for commands on the Ribbon. The tab names appear at the top of the Ribbon and the active tab appears in front.

Text annotations Labels added to a chart to draw attention to or describe a particular area.

Text concatenation operators In a formula, symbols used to join strings of text in different cells.

Theme A predefined set of colors, fonts, line and fill effects, and other formats that can be applied to an Excel worksheet and give it a consistent, professional look.

Tick marks Notations of a scale of measure on a chart axis.

Title bar Appears at the top of every Office program window; displays the document name and program name.

User interface A collective term for all the ways you interact with a software program.

Value axis In a chart, the axis that contains numerical values; in a 2-dimensional chart, also known as the y-axis.

Values Numbers, formulas, and functions used in calculations.

View A method of displaying a document window to show more or fewer details or a different combination of elements that makes it easier to complete certain tasks, such as formatting or reading text.

Web Note In Microsoft Edge, an annotation on a webpage.

What-if analysis A decision-making tool in which data is changed and formulas are recalculated, in order to predict various possible outcomes.

Workbook A collection of related worksheets contained within a single file which has the file extension xlsx.

Worksheet A single sheet within a workbook file; also, the entire area within an electronic spreadsheet that contains a grid of columns and rows.

Worksheet window Area of the program window that displays part of the current worksheet; the worksheet window displays only a small fraction of the worksheet, which can contain a total of 1,048,576 rows and 16,384 columns.

X-axis The horizontal axis in a chart; because it often shows data categories, such as months or locations, *also called* Category axis.

XML Acronym that stands for eXtensible Markup Language, which is a language used to structure, store, and send information.

Y-axis The vertical axis in a chart; because it often shows numerical values, *also called* Value axis.

Z-axis The third axis in a true 3-D chart, lets you compare data points across both categories and values.

Zooming in A feature that makes a document appear larger but shows less of it on screen at once; does not affect actual document size.

Zooming out A feature that shows more of a document on screen at once but at a reduced size; does not affect actual document size.

Index